Purr-ables from Heaven

M.R WELLS
DOTTIE P. ADAMS
CONNIE FLEISHAUER

HARVEST HOUSE PUBLISHERS
EUGENE, OREGON

Published in association with the literary agency of Mark Sweeney & Associates, 28540 Altessa Way, Ste. 201, Bonita Springs, FL 34135

Cover by Left Coast Design, Portland, Oregon

Cover photo © GK Hart / Vikki Hart / The Image Bank / Getty Images

The information shared by the authors is from their personal experience and should not be considered professional advice. Readers should consult their own cat care professionals regarding issues related to the health, safety, grooming, and training of their pets.

PURR-ABLES FROM HEAVEN

Published by Harvest House Publishers
Eugene, Oregon 97402
www.harvesthousepublishers.com

Library of Congress Cataloging-in-Publication Data
Wells, M. R. (Marion R.), 1948-
Purr-ables from heaven / M.R. Wells, Connie Fleishauer, and Dottie P. Adams.
p. cm.
ISBN-13: 978-0-7369-2057-5 (pbk.)
ISBN-10: 0-7369-2057-9
1. Cat owners—Prayers and devotions. 2. Cats—Religious aspects—Christianity. I. Fleishauer, Connie. II. Adams, Dottie P., 1944- III. Title.
BV4596.A54W46 2008
242—dc22

2007019416

Printed in the United States of America

08 09 10 11 12 13 14 15 16 / VP-SK / 12 11 10 9 8 7 6 5 4

We joyfully dedicate this book to the cats and humans we hold dear, and to the Author of our faith, who called us to the task. Thank You, Lord, for keeping the promise You made at the start: "Be strong and courageous, and do the work. Do not be afraid or discouraged, for the LORD God, my God, is with you. He will not fail you or forsake you" (1 Chronicles 28:20).

Acknowledgments

Birthing a book is rarely, if ever, a solo effort. Ours is truly a product of the body of Christ. So many wonderful people prayed for us, supported us, and let us share their stories. We want to thank our families, our friends, our prayer and Bible study groups, and our churches for all they have done to uplift and uphold us. We're also grateful to our feline families for their irreplaceable contributions to this book and to our lives.

Special thanks to our agents, Mark and Janet Sweeney, for all their efforts on our behalf; to Paige Evans, DVM, for her comments and suggestions on our manuscript; to Stephanie Smolinski, for her title idea; and to our marvelous team at Harvest House Publishers, especially our awesome editor, Kim Moore. Most of all, we thank and praise God, without whom this book could not have been written and would have no reason to be. We gladly give Him all honor and glory, now and forever!

Contents

Part 1
Let's Get Purr-sonal
God Draws Us to Himself

Part II
Stretching Exercises
God Stimulates Our Growth

Part III
To Hiss or Not to Hiss?
God Cleanses and Refines Us

Part IV
Scratching Post Guidance
God Teaches Us His Ways

Part V
Who's Top Cat?
God Reigns over Us for Our Good

Foreword

The ancient Egyptians got it all wrong. They revered, even worshipped, cats. God wasn't too pleased, but we doubt the cats minded. They probably lapped up all the adulation they were given. They're still doing so today.

Actually, we humans were born to have dominion over all other creatures and worship the Creator we share. But our kitties don't always get that straight, and neither do we. Perhaps that's what makes them such a marvelous mirror to reflect our own foibles and God's care and love for us in spite of them.

Cats are a study in contradictions. By turns they're endearing and exasperating; adoring and aloof; pliable and petulant. When they give their affection, it means that much more because they can be such little rebels too. Even as we tear out our hair because of them, we laugh at their antics and hand them our hearts. Even as they're declaring their independence, we are pledging our allegiance.

Ah, what a wonderful picture of our relationship with God. We are contradictory, willful creatures also. Yet God not only bears with us, He sent His Son to die that we might be redeemed to spend eternity with Him. We are grateful to our kitties for giving us a glimpse of ourselves from God's perspective, and a window into His great love for us and patience with us. We pray our stories may spur you to delight in the Lord and curl up in His lap.

BARNEY

MISTY

KITTY

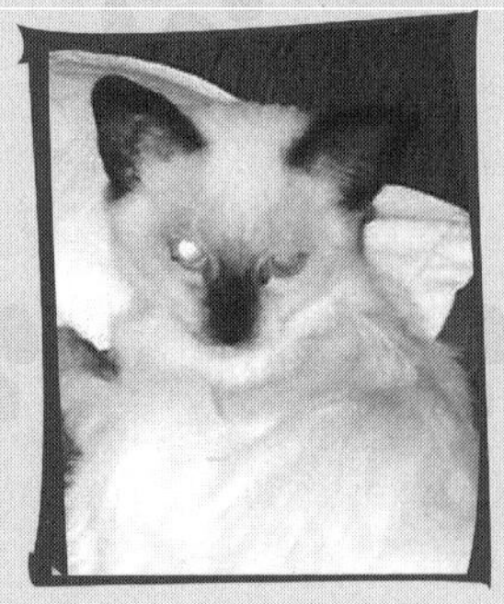

WALLY

MOOCH

PUMPKIN

MUFFIN

MERLIN

MILKSHAKE

MIDNIGHT

TIGER

Meet the Kitties

Wells Cats

PRIMARY PLAYERS

BARNEY has the deep chocolate coat and green eyes of the breed called Havana Brown, although his lineage is mixed. At 19, he's my oldest cat—and my biggest talker. When he was younger, he used to spring to a perch high atop a kitchen cabinet to snooze or survey his world. These days he's so stiff he settles for a low stool. But though his body is faltering, his will is as strong as ever. He meows for his due and won't quit—a perfect illustration of "persistence in prayer."

MISTY is a beautiful blue point Birman, also in the twilight of her life. Small of stature, she has a huge spirit and has never let larger cats intimidate her. She can curl up for hours at a time by herself, but she welcomes attention when she's in the mood. She will lick my hair in an effort to groom me and curl up on my chest to be petted—as long as it happens on her terms and timing. This old girl demands respect.

MUFFIN is a fluffy seal point Ragdoll who loves to wind humans around her paw. She looks like a princess and acts like one too. When she first joined my family, my two dogs became her surrogate parents, and she adores them to this day. She loves to climb on my lap in the morning and snuggle and purr while I have my coffee, or flop atop the cat tree in my office. She's spunky and playful, batting paper balls and diving after the small round shadow of my watch face as if it were a mouse.

MERLIN was a longhaired orange tabby I got from a rescue group. He had the loudest purr in the house. "Big Red" knew no strangers and sported a strong macho streak. He once tried to leap from the top of the fridge to a cabinet above the oven in a single bound. This good-natured guy was "all boy" and played hard. He pounced on Muffin with such vigor she shrieked. But he meant no harm—because, big as he was, his heart was bigger still.

GUEST CAST

KITTY and RANGER were my first-ever cats whom I coaxed to step onto the "porch of trust." They star in "The Taming of Cats and Humans."

FLUFFY was a childhood kitty who preferred fur to puffed sleeves. She stars in "A Cat in Doll's Clothing."

BO is my newest cat and God's reminder that miracles happen. He stars in "Jericho Moments."

EZEKIEL (ZEKE) belonged to a housemate and lived up to his biblical name. He stars in "Saved by a Watchcat."

BONCO was my mom's "mellow yellow" kitty who let birds steal his meal. He stars in "Great Expectations."

LEIA is a friend's "teenage" cat, named for the famous *Star Wars* character. She stars in "Separation Anxiety."

Fleishauer Cats

PRIMARY PLAYERS

KITTY was a beautiful black cat with white on her tail and paws. She mothered not just her own kittens, but others. She also tried to protect her people, following our family all over our farm up to her own personal boundary lines. But when we moved, she couldn't get used to our new home and went back to her old haunts.

WALLY was a fluffy longhaired kitten with both light and dark brown shadings. She was born on our roof and fell into a hole between the walls. Her mama gave her up for dead, but our family did not. We rescued her, and this tiny little spitfire touched our hearts and lives.

MILKSHAKE was a beautiful black-and-white cat our granddaughter adopted as her very own. He knew he was special to her and basked in her love. Braver than his peers, he feasted on food other kitties feared to taste and made friends with the dog who would have chased him from our yard.

GUEST CAST

MACEE was a childhood cat who nearly brought a holiday crashing down. She stars in "Christmas Treed."

UNO and DOS were twin cats from my youth who literally couldn't live without each other. They star in "Uno, Dos, Grace."

TABBY was my husband's youthful pet whose focus was "on the ball." She stars in "Tabby's Mission."

KELLY was a beautiful calico cat who hated to lift a paw, preferring to laze the day away. She stars in "A Time to Work."

CHESTER, LESTER, and WEBSTER were orphans who came "out of their shell" for some caring kids. They star in "Jumping from the Helmet."

RAJAH was a kitten who loved to pose. She stars in "Picture Purr-fect."

LUCY was a boy cat we first thought was a girl, who submitted to a bath we thought he would fight. He stars in "Grease."

SWEETIE was a lost little kitten who longed for acceptance and persevered. She stars in "All in the Family."

MICHELIN missed a legacy, so her kittens ran from humans too. She stars in "Legacy Lost."

BEAMER and CHEVY belong to our daughter Christy—and her alone. They star in "Totally Yours."

Adams Cats

PRIMARY PLAYERS

MIDNIGHT is a jet black cat with green eyes. She's the wildest kitty we have ever known. She's so easily stimulated, our vet even offered to put her on Prozac. In one split second, she can go from purring in ecstasy to pouncing on the hand that motivated the purrs. Now that she's ten and slowing a bit, the mice, birds, and insects in our yard are breathing a bit easier. But when she patrols her domain, she still reminds us of a panther on the prowl.

MOOCH is a four-year-old gray tabby with beautiful white highlights on his face, chest, and paws. We inherited him from a dear church friend who went to be with Jesus. Mooch's sweet disposition made it easy to fall in love with him. He plays with toys more than any other cat we've had and is quite a catcher. He loves hanging out with us and hates being put to bed at night.

PUMPKIN was a beautiful, mellow orange tabby named by our then six-year-old daughter. Born in our bedroom, he seemed happy every minute of his nearly 20 years. He loved other cats and people and greeted visitors to our home as if he were the master of it, not us. Better than any welcome mat, our "welcome cat" won the hearts of one and all.

TIGER was Pumpkin's sister, but her coloring was quite different. She was gray with blue eyes and a beautiful bronze belly. Her exceptionally sweet disposition made her my husband's all-time favorite cat. Every night she slept between us, purring us to sleep if we touched her. Tiger was as much of a chicken as Pumpkin was personable. She loved her family but feared all others—serving as a living illustration of the term "scaredy-cat."

GUEST STARS

RACKY was the one cat we allowed to get pregnant. She stars in "The Miracle of Birth."

TASHA didn't look like the most ideal pet, but loving eyes saw her potential. She stars in "Caged or Free?"

Part I

Let's Get Purr-sonal

God Draws Us to Himself

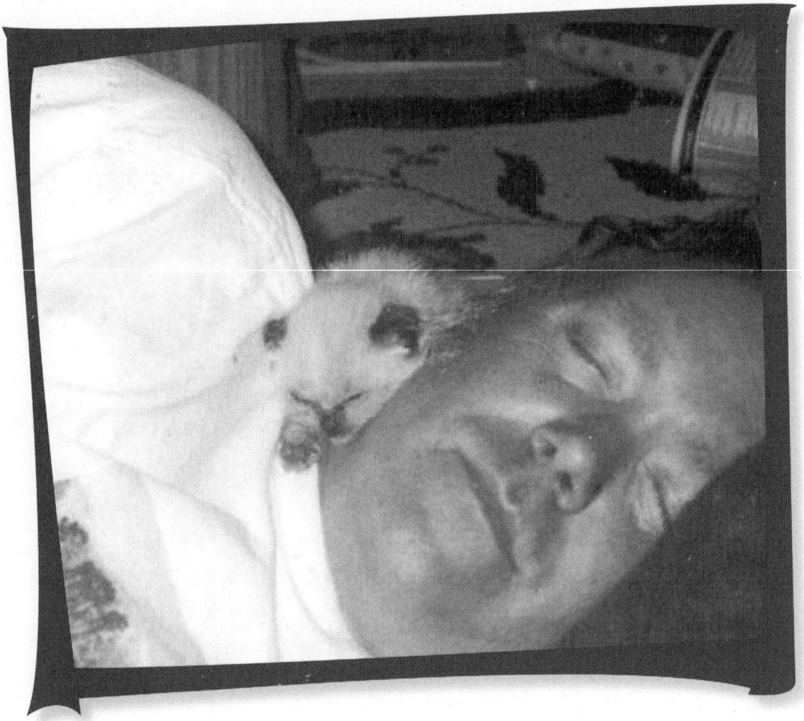

WALLY

Wally on Our Shoulders

Curl Up on God's Lap

The eternal God is your refuge, and
underneath are the everlasting arms.

Deuteronomy 33:27

Wally was our tiniest kitten, but she gave us many big lessons. She ran the whole family for a while, small as she was. Whenever any of us would come home, the first thing we would do is look for her. We wanted to hold her—but we also didn't want to step on her.

When we were sitting in the living room, Wally usually perched on someone's lap, or better yet, their shoulders. My husband Steve's broad shoulders were a favorite spot. She would roll into a little ball and fall asleep far above her world. She didn't seem at all afraid to be up there. In fact, this was where she seemed to feel most comfortable and safe.

Steve's lap was where our children felt most comfortable and safe when they were young. It seemed no one could harm them when they were sitting there. Dad's lap was their place to relax when they were tired or frustrated.

Christy was four when John was two. She liked to play quietly with her toys. He liked to throw them. Christy would labor to draw a pretty picture on her Etch A Sketch. When she was just about finished, John would grab it and throw it across the room. Christy would cry and run to her daddy for safety. Steve would hold her and her toys in his lap till John lost interest and went on to the next thing.

John played hard and got hurt more often than our girls. He'd come in complaining about a skinned knee or elbow he got riding—or more accurately, crashing—his bike. He'd sit on Daddy's lap while I got the first aid kit to fix him up. Dad's lap was a good place to rest. It was also a good hangar when John was pretending he was an airplane.

Our younger daughter Karen spent lots of time on Steve's lap too. She would set up her little tea set and serve him pretend tea. She would climb up on his lap and they would enjoy their pretend tea with real cookies. She felt like a queen sitting on a throne.

All our children loved to be on Steve's lap when he read to them. They would fight for the coveted lap position. One child would prevail and the others had to settle for sitting beside him, but everyone was contented and happy.

I believe our children found Steve's lap so comforting because Steve found comfort in his heavenly Father. He knew what it was to seek solace on God's lap. Steve was only 23 years old when I gave birth to our first babies, Erin and Stephen. I was in labor for at least four days. He stayed with me until he was so sleep deprived he couldn't think straight. When he went home at last and fell into bed exhausted, he felt his heavenly Father's arms around him. God continued to uphold him, and all of us, when our babies died and we had to make arrangements for their burial.

I have imagined myself sitting in God's lap many times in my life. One of these was when I went back to college to finish my degree. My children were still in school themselves. I remember how hard it was to keep up with all the other demands in my life and yet go to classes and do homework. It was almost more than I could handle. Many times I would come home, drop in my chair, put up my feet, close my eyes, and imagine myself dropping all the stuff of life at my heavenly Father's feet and curling up in His lap. I could almost feel His wonderful loving arms encircle me as He stroked my hair and told me He loved me.

In Deuteronomy 33, Moses blessed the tribes of Israel. When it came to Benjamin, he said, "Let the beloved of the LORD rest secure in him, for he shields him all day long, and the one the LORD loves rests between his shoulders" (Deuteronomy 33:12).

We are God's children. We're beloved by Him. We can rest on our Master's shoulders, just as Wally did. We can climb into our Father's lap, just as Karen and Christy and John climbed into Steve's. When life's burdens grow heavy, we can run to Him and find refuge and comfort and strength to go on in the loving embrace of His everlasting arms.

Praise be to the God and Father of our Lord Jesus Christ, the Father of compassion and the God of all comfort, who comforts us in all our troubles, so that we can comfort those in any trouble with the comfort we ourselves have received from God (2 Corinthians 1:3-4).

Consider This

Have you ever felt overwhelmed and sought refuge in God's lap? Did you feel comforted? Protected? Loved? Did this make your relationship with your heavenly Father more intimate? If so, how?

Storm Warnings

God Is Our Refuge

I am not afraid of storms, for I am learning how to sail my ship.

Louisa May Alcott

I live in Los Angeles, where it doesn't usually rain a lot. But "usual" wasn't happening in February 2005. The city not only exceeded its normal rainfall, it even topped that of Seattle, Washington, by ten inches. And the rainy season had barely begun. Not only that, but it wasn't a gentle kind of rain. It was a furious kind, with lightning and thunder.

One night the rain was pounding so hard it roused me at 2 a.m. Because I was wide awake, I decided to check up on Midnight. She's such a nervous little cat that she sometimes reminds me of a cartoon character when she leaps backward, eyes wide with fright and fur standing on end. She loves the guest bedroom and normally spends the night on the bed, curled up in a tight little ball with her head resting on the pillow as if she were human. Perhaps she thinks she is.

This night, however, she crouched under the bed, looking utterly terrified. I petted her a bit and then returned to my own room. I had just become cozy and warm and drowsy enough to fall back to sleep when I heard a foreign sound. It was hail hammering down on our house.

We live only three miles from the Pacific Ocean in a temperate climate, so hail makes the news. I got up once more and went downstairs to have a look outside. It was remarkable to see the backyard deck covered with little white balls bouncing all over the place. I decided to look out front as well. When I opened the door, the noise was deafening. Taken aback, I retreated from the doorway. That's when I saw Midnight, crawling as low to the floor as she could possibly get. It seemed as if she were moving in slow motion as she wandered in circles, wondering where to go to get away from this horror. She had come downstairs in search of relief, but it was just as scary here as upstairs, and she didn't know where to turn or what to do.

I knelt and tried to reassure her that in spite of the noise, everything was okay. But she was not to be consoled. She let me pet her, but her eyes were as big as saucers as she stared frantically around the room. As I stroked her soft fur I thought about how God tries to console me amid my own fearful events.

I was 45 years old when my husband suffered a heart attack. The pain in his upper back had begun in the early morning, but he thought it was just a muscle he had pulled while exercising. When the pain continued he became more concerned, but he made it through the workday. On the drive home it grew so intense that he headed for the hospital our family used. When he realized he might not make it, he pulled into a gas station and asked that they call 911. The ambulance drivers took him to a hospital I had never heard of.

At home I knew something was wrong because Phil was always on time. He was so punctual you could set your clock by him. I began to pray and then called a friend, who dropped everything to come and stay with me. When the hospital finally called, she drove me there.

At first the doctors diagnosed him with pericarditis, an inflammation of the sac around the heart. But when his blood work came back, the diagnosis changed to a heart attack. Phil had a blocked artery that needed to be opened. Our personal doctor had him transferred to our close hospital because it had a cardiac unit. Once he had an angioplasty that got the blood flowing in his artery again, we knew he would survive. Phil said he felt as if he could get up and run home. Relief flooded over me like the sun breaking through on a cold, foggy day. I was so thankful I could hardly stop talking about it.

However, though life around me soon returned to normal, I didn't. Usually I love to have devotions with the Lord each morning. I imagine we are both having a cup of coffee together as I pray and study His Word. These days I just had coffee. When I tried to pray I knew I was only going through the motions, for my heart wasn't in it. I was tempted to stop going to my desk at all. I wished I could sleep more, but I was too agitated. Nothing consoled me and I felt confused, the way Midnight did as she ran in circles. I was too afraid to believe that everything really was okay. Phil had lost a lot of heart muscle, and I had lost a lot of trust in my Jesus. There was a storm in my heart that had me as confused as the one Midnight experienced.

I spent two uncomfortable months like this. Finally, I realized I must tell my feelings to the Lord. I sat down that morning and wrote Him a letter. I told Him I felt that I couldn't trust Him anymore, that I was disappointed in what He had allowed, and that I was afraid my life would never be the same.

The difference between my response and Midnight's is that she was not consoled until the storm moved on; she couldn't settle down until the hail stopped. Her consolation was dependent upon her circumstances. Mine needn't be. I have a Savior who not only wants to comfort me, but also wants to help me understand what

I'm feeling and walk through the storm with me, if I will allow Him to do so.

My fears about my circumstances had stopped my communication with God. Once I brought them to Jesus, He reassured me that because He was still sovereign, everything really was okay. He would never leave me, and even if I left Him, He'd be waiting for me to come back because He was just like the prodigal's father. He wanted me to do what 1 Peter 5:7 tells us to do, "Cast all your anxiety on him because he cares for you."

He never promised to change my circumstances, but He did promise to be with me in and through them. As time passed, I wondered if my Lord felt as I did when I tried unsuccessfully to comfort Midnight on the night of the storm. I had wanted desperately to help her. In the same way, I believe God was there, desiring to help me in my distress, but I wouldn't let Him in.

Jesus said He is knocking at the door, but we must choose whether to open to Him. He is telling this to believers. When we refuse, we rob ourselves of His loving care. The next time I'm caught in a storm and feel as though I'm running in circles in my circumstances, I pray I will throw my heart open and run straight to His arms.

Here I am! I stand at the door and knock. If anyone hears my voice and opens the door, I will come in and eat with him, and he with me (Revelation 3:20).

Consider This

When were you last in the middle of a storm? If you ran in circles in your circumstances, what was the result? If you let the Lord in, how did He comfort you? Do you need to open the door and ask Jesus to come into your life and circumstances right now?

Let There Be Peace

Our Peace Is in God

Peace is not the absence of affliction, but the presence of God.

Author Unknown

With five children and two parents living in one small home, Mom was never too keen on letting pets inside. Outside was "where animals belong." My cat Macee stayed mostly in our backyard. But on rare occasions she was allowed to come into the den when one of us needed special treatment.

I remember holding Macee when I was sick and home from school. She would sit peacefully on my lap for hours. It was as though she knew I needed her special calming effect in my life just at that moment. She also helped Mom out by keeping me quietly busy.

Macee brought Mom the gift of peace in other ways. Mom seemed to enjoy certain outside chores. She'd work in the yard, sometimes singing songs to her heavenly Father. Macee would come and sit next to her. After a while, she'd stop and pet my sweet, gentle cat. The two were a picture of peace.

Not all animals in our life had a calming effect on Mom, though. One in particular caused great chaos. We had wonderful neighbors and friends on our left. They were outdoor people who loved to hunt and fish. They also loved animals. Cats and dogs were not enough for these friends. Somewhere on a journey of theirs, they found and purchased a little spider monkey.

Sammy the monkey seemed happy enough, but he was hardly content to stay peacefully in his cage. He tried hard to escape and investigate the rest of the world. His favorite "rest of the world" was our peaceful backyard. When he got out, he would swing down the length of our clothesline, getting our cat and dog all in a dither. Macee hissed and spat. Our dog barked and jumped to catch him—but Sammy was much too quick.

It was fun to watch this little backyard circus—unless Mom was outside too. She was terribly frightened of Sammy, and he seemed to know it. When he saw her, he'd head straight for her across the clothesline, making a bloodcurdling noise. She would scream, throw the clothes in the air and race inside, slamming the door and yelling, "I hate that monkey!" Any of us who were home would double over laughing until we cried.

Sammy would stay by the door for a while, watching Mom check to see if he'd left yet. When he was finally gone, she would go back outside and finish her chores. Macee would often join her. I don't know if Mom ever cried on our cat's furry shoulder, but I can just imagine what Mom might have said if she did: "Oh, that horrible monkey! Why must he turn my day upside down? Why can't he be gentle and peaceful, like you are?"

While Macee sometimes brought Mom a few moments of peace, Mom found her true peace in God. Mom knew Jesus Christ as her personal Savior. She and Dad taught us kids that Jesus is the Prince of Peace, and that if we gave our lives to Him, we could have His peace regardless of our circumstances.

Looking back, I see Sammy the monkey as a metaphor for the chaos the world and its tribulations can bring. Macee is a picture of the peace God can give us in the midst of our circumstances. God offers us peace with Him through faith in Christ's death for our sins, and He offers us peace amid life's trials by trusting in His care. Jesus told His disciples, "Peace I leave with you; my peace I give you. I do not give to you as the world gives. Do not let your hearts be troubled and do not be afraid" (John 14:27).

Our precious neighbor and his wife have been gone from this world many years now, but they will never leave our hearts. I believe that God put us in their lives—just as He put Macee in our family's life—to offer gifts of peace. Everyone is searching for peace—both for themselves and for the world at large. God offers that peace, but we must choose whether to receive it.

Jesus said, "Blessed are the peacemakers, for they will be called sons of God" (Matthew 5:9). God calls His children to be peacemakers and tell others about the gifts of peace He offers so all will know that true peace is found only in Him.

May the God of hope fill you with all joy and peace as you trust in him, so that you may overflow with hope by the power of the Holy Spirit (Romans 15:13).

Consider This

What in your life is most likely to disturb your peace? What is most likely to restore it? Has God given you peace in the midst of trials or chaos? How did He do so? How might you be an instrument of God's peace to someone else?

Midnight Meows the Blues

God Heals the Brokenhearted

God didn't promise days without pain,
laughter without sorrow, sun without rain,
but He did promise strength for the day,
comfort for the tears, and light for the way.

Author Unknown

I didn't know cats could be depressed. Yet Midnight was showing all the signs: sleeping more than usual, having less energy, being less interested in her world. Clearly, our black cat was feeling blue. Even her eyes looked sad.

My husband, Phil, pinpointed the cause. "Midnight misses Pumpkin. She'll be okay in a few weeks." Our wonderful orange tabby, Pumpkin, had been her mentor, playmate, and companion. She'd bonded with Pumpkin as a kitten. She would chase Pumpkin in the yard until he suddenly leaped up and spun around to become her pursuer. On rainy days, she'd curl up with Pumpkin. And Pumpkin had just died. It made sense that she was grieving.

Phil's words were prophetic. It took Midnight about five weeks to return to normal. In the meantime, we took special care of her.

We spent extra time each day petting her and talking to her. We told her how much we loved her and how precious she was. We would sit near her, and we'd give her little treats to say, "We're with you, Midnight."

As we ministered to Midnight in her loss, I recalled a time when I'd been depressed because of missing people close to me. Our oldest son and his family had moved 300 miles away. They'd been living in our home while our son earned his master's degree. Blending families has its challenges, but I felt we did very well. My great joy was in helping to care for my two grandsons, one of whom was born while they lived with us.

They originally planned to settle close by us after the schooling was done, so I imagined this kind of life would continue. I thought we'd be like the family my son had joined when he was away at college. They had gathered for a weekly meal, after which all the grandchildren spent the night. To me, as a grandma, that sounded idyllic. I also envisioned attending swim lessons, school plays, and church pageants. The future, in my mind, was completely mapped out, and it was glorious!

However, none of that was meant to be. Perhaps because I had allowed my imagination full reign, it became even more difficult to cope with the reality of them leaving. Their departure shattered my dreams and broke my heart completely. I became depressed.

As Midnight had done, I slept more and lacked energy. Unlike Midnight, I cried every day. But I had the blessing of being in the Bible constantly—because I teach a Bible study class. We were in the Gospel of John that year, and that was where God healed me.

My study of Jesus as the Passover Lamb sacrificed for the sins of the world (Isaiah 53:7 and John 1:29) helped me to give up that little family as a sacrifice in my own life. I was able to get in line with God's will, not my own. I began to say over and over to myself, "Sometimes life isn't good, but God is good all the time."

I forced myself to go outside and sit in the sun each day. As I did, I would invite the Son to be with me. As I meditated on Jesus being the light of the world (John 8:12), the darkness I felt would lift for a time. Just as the sun warmed my outsides, the Son warmed my soul. I knew I was being healed.

As I meditated on Jesus saying, "I am the resurrection and the life" (John 11:25), it dawned on me that I needed to trust in resurrection power to save me. God still had a plan for my life. It just wasn't my plan. I added a new thought to my daily meditations: "For a Christian there is always the promise of resurrection." Old dreams had died. Now I needed new dreams to rise in the life God had planned for me.

Jesus never reprimanded me for being depressed. Instead, He treated me in much the same way we treated Midnight during her hard time. He drew close and comforted my heart. He gave me little touches of Himself as I walked through those months of suffering. Even the fact that I was deeply involved in the Gospel of John felt like a kiss from heaven. God knew what I needed even before it happened.

My son's precious family now lives 800 miles away, but we are as emotionally close as when they lived in our home. I still wish they were in my city, but I'm comforted knowing they are where God wants them, doing His will.

I was healed during those months, and God became more real to me. I wouldn't want to repeat the suffering, but I wouldn't want to have missed God's touch, either. Through that painful time, I gained a deeper understanding of His tender care, not just for me, but for all His children who are hurting.

The Lord is close to the brokenhearted and saves those who are crushed in spirit (Psalm 34:18).

CONSIDER THIS

Have you felt God's special care during a hard time in your life? What did He do? How did it help you heal? How might you encourage someone else who's going through a tough time?

Chosen Ones

God Adopts Us As His Own

Adoption is when a child grew in its mommy's heart instead of her tummy.

Author Unknown

The old farm home was rather quiet now. It had seen three generations of Fleishauers growing up within its walls. Now only Karen lived there with my husband, Steve, and me. But our older children, Christy and John, came home often to share a meal and life's adventures.

Then, life changed.

John called one day to tell us he was dating a wonderful girl named Sari. She was a Christian and a high school teacher, and she had a little girl named Sierra. When he brought them over to meet us the next day, it was easy to see that Sari was holding John's heart. Sierra made herself right at home, and we felt as if she belonged. When we hugged goodbye, I felt assured that this was the beginning of the fourth generation of our family.

On her next visit, Sierra fell in love with the newest generation of our animal family—Kitty's latest litter of kittens. We knew she couldn't take one home with her because of her allergy to cats. But her mom said she could adopt one to keep at our house and care for it when she came to see us.

Sierra looked carefully at each kitten. She held each one and petted it. Finally she chose Bo to be her own, and renamed him Milkshake. Now whenever she came over, Sierra looked for Milkshake first thing. She would hold him and pet him and tell him how much she loved him. Before long, Milkshake would run up to Sierra the moment she got out of the car. He followed her all over the yard and house. It was fun to watch him and see how well the two got along. Milkshake turned from a shy little kitty into one who loved to play and be in the arms of his owner, Sierra. Milkshake knew that Sierra loved him. His desire was to be near her at all times. Her desire was to love and care for him.

John married Sari. And although he was not Sierra's legal father, their hearts connected and he was her daddy. John's love for Sierra was evident to her as he cared for her. Now when we heard of John's adventures, they included Sierra's softball games, soccer games, and other activities. John took Sari and Sierra riding in the desert and loved teaching Sierra to drive a special sand vehicle called a quad. When Sierra won second place in her school's science fair, John was beaming with pride for his little girl.

Because Sierra's birth father hadn't been involved in her life for quite some time, John wanted to adopt her as soon as possible. He was willing to do whatever it took. He had to go through a rigorous background check. He was interviewed, as were many who knew him. Their day in court was filled with smiles, hugs, and happy tears from all the family on both sides when the adoption was finalized at last.

Sierra has another adopted Daddy—God. He also did whatever it took to adopt her—and all His children. He sent His Son, Jesus, to save us from sin. Jesus went to court, was falsely convicted, died, was buried, and then He rose again and is preparing a place for us in heaven if we accept Him as our personal Savior.

One day I asked Sierra why she'd invited Jesus into her heart. She told me that she wanted a heavenly Father. She knew He had protected her mom and herself. She said she loved God and knew He loved her because He answered her prayers. She'd realized she couldn't have a cat at home, but she'd really wanted one, and God gave her Milkshake. She'd prayed for a daddy and someone for her mom to love, and God gave them John. Now Sierra is going to a special program at church which helps her learn Bible verses and understand more about her Abba (Daddy) in heaven and what it means to be His child.

Milkshake and Sierra didn't earn their adoption. We can't earn ours, either. But God offers it to all of us as a gift because He loves us. If we receive it, we will forever enjoy all the rights and privileges of being His child.

Praise be to the God and Father of our Lord Jesus Christ, who has blessed us in the heavenly realms with every spiritual blessing in Christ. For he chose us in him before the creation of the world to be holy and blameless in his sight. In love he predestined us to be adopted as his sons through Jesus Christ, in accordance with his pleasure and will—to the praise of his glorious grace, which he has freely given us in the One he loves (Ephesians 1:3-6).

CONSIDER THIS

Have you ever adopted a kitty or other pet? How did you

care for and love it, and how did it respond? Have you ever adopted a child or known someone who did? What was their experience? Have you ever been adopted by God? If so, how has God expressed His love and care for you? If not, what is keeping you from accepting His offer of adoption?

Totally Yours

Delight in the Lord

Our only business is to love and
delight ourselves in God.

Brother Lawrence

Chevy and Beamer belong to our daughter Christy. She took them to live with her in her sweet little house across town. As far as people go, they love only Christy. When she gets home, they are waiting to greet her. If she lies on the sofa, they sit near her or in her lap, basking in her presence. They follow her around the house and sleep with her at night. They stay close every morning while she's getting ready for work. Chevy perches on the bathroom counter and meows her little kitty talk, as if to say, "Christy, I love you." When Christy acknowledges her and pets her, Chevy jumps down and walks away contented. Beamer sits on the windowsill and towel rack, watching her master until she's done dressing. Then they both follow her to the door to get a final pat on the head and an "I love you" before Christy leaves for the day.

Christy's kitties don't give such adoration to anyone else. When others come over, they run and hide. If Christy's away, we feed them and try to give them some attention, but they stay out of sight the whole time we're there. Christy would like them to come out and play with us, but they won't.

Clearly, these kitties are devoted to Christy. No one can take her place with them. They are totally hers. They worship her.

I don't worship my husband, Steve, but no one can take his place with me. I am totally his and I love him more than anyone else in this world. We met as teens and have been married more than 34 years. I like to say we've been married for most of our lives. He is my companion, confidant, lover, soul mate, and best friend.

Steve and I love being together. I'll join him in activities I'd never do on my own. He loves to go bass fishing. Sometimes I tag along. I sit with my line in the water and talk to the fish. Sometimes I also sing quietly to them. Now and then I catch one. Steve checks his graphs, studies the water, puts just the right plastic worm on his line, and casts it in a particular place. He catches fish much more often.

I enjoy fishing with Steve, but it's not because of the fishing. I go to be with him. I love to be in his presence. Catching fish is a plus.

I also feel a deep connection with Steve when he plays his trumpet on our praise team at church. When he's with the band, he sits right in front of me. I feel a deep three-way bond between Steve, myself, and the Lord when he plays and we sing praises to our heavenly Father.

Steve is sensitive to my needs, just as Christy is to Chevy's and Beamer's. When we have guests for dinner, he pitches in with housecleaning and cooking. If I need extra help with something, he seems to notice right away and rushes to my aid. He loves me and takes care of me—just as Christy cares for her cats.

I have other people in my life who also try to meet some of my needs, but they aren't special in the same way Steve is. They can't take his place. He is my lover and provider in a way they aren't. Other than my Lord and Savior, I love no one more than I love him.

I love and worship the triune God—Father, Son, and Holy Spirit. No one else can take His place with me. No one else can fill any of His titles. God alone is my Creator. Christ alone is my Lord and Savior. Still, there are times when I am not totally His. There are moments when I put something else ahead of Him, and I'm sure this makes Him sad.

I did this with singing. When I was younger, I was often asked to sing solos. Almost every group I sang in was made up of believers. I would feel competitive toward other soloists. I came to realize I was putting my ego ahead of my relationship with God. I knew this grieved Him. I confessed—both to God and to my fellow singers. It wasn't easy, but it restored the joy of my relationship with my Master.

God wants us to be totally His. He wants to love and care for us, as He did by showing me how singing needs to fit into my life. And even when I let something else interfere with my closeness to Him, perhaps something as simple as too much television, He is eager to take me back.

Christy delights in Chevy and Beamer and basks in their love and adoration. Steve delights to know that I love him best and I am totally his. God delights in us too. We can't even begin to conceive of the love He has for us. He is waiting and longing to fellowship with us. So be totally His, bask in His love, and delight yourself in Him.

The LORD your God is with you, he is mighty to save. He will take great delight in you, he will quiet you with his love, he will rejoice over you with singing (Zephaniah 3:17).

CONSIDER THIS

Do you delight yourself in the Lord? If so, how do you show love for Him? What are some ways you've experienced His love for you? If delighting in Him isn't a priority, what is keeping you from being totally His?

Caged or Free?

God's Love Is Key

If we treat people as they are, we make them worse. If we treat people as they ought to be, we help them become what they are capable of becoming.

Johann Wolfgang von Goethe

Tasha lay contentedly on the back of the sofa, unaffected by the commotion in her busy household. Even flying toys didn't seem to bother her, nor did the dogs' noses as they sniffed this new addition to their family. Nothing could disturb her now. She was free of the cage she'd been locked in so long and had her own home at last.

Tasha was a longhaired tortoiseshell cat, somewhere around two years old. No one knew where she'd spent the first year of her life. They only knew that for the past five months, she'd been kept in a cage at a pet store. Other cats and dogs had too, but she'd spent the longest time there.

Probably that was because Tasha seemed undesirable, at least in appearance. Her long fur was full of mats and tangles, she had to be dewormed, and she wasn't very communicative. People coming in for a kitty either chose younger ones or verbal ones whose meows seemed to say, "Take me. I'll be the perfect pet."

So Tasha remained in her cage, the cat "not taken"—until the day my friend Grace spied her. Grace looked beyond the tangles and mats and saw a cat who needed her. It was love at first sight. All she had to do was convince her husband to welcome another pet into their household of twin daughters and two dogs. To Grace's delight, Tasha tugged at his heart too. Within weeks of coming home, their new cat was curling up contentedly in both their laps. She was free at last.

Grace had been in her own cage when she was very young. Her mother left the family when Grace was an infant and was out of Grace's life for the next nine years. Though her father was a friendly man, he had rage issues, so she was hit a lot as a child for doing normal childish things. Then her mom returned and took her to another city. But that situation brought other challenges because her mother had a drinking problem. So Grace spent much of her time alone or at a school friend's house.

In her teens, one particular Christian family took Grace in for weeks at a time. Because of their kindness, she began to see what a healthy family was like. It became her dream to have that kind of family someday, a family she considered "normal." As she imagined her future life, it included a kind, caring husband, many kids, and a home of her own.

The Christian family's walk with Jesus and willingness to take her in so often taught Grace what Christianity was all about. It wasn't just people going to a church building once a week. It was a lifestyle of love, prayer, forgiveness, openness, and sharing with those who had a need—all because of the love of Jesus. Grace became great friends with the daughter of this wonderful family, and she not only heard the gospel that Jesus was alive and ready to help anyone who came to Him, but she also saw the gospel being lived out as this family loved and cared for her.

Grace received Jesus as a young adult and was rescued from the cage of sin we're all locked in until Christ sets us free. She began to ask God for the life she had only dreamed about when she was in the cage. She also prayed for the right man to share her new life with her.

Grace met the man God had for her one night at work. Two years later they were married. God knew exactly who to bring for Grace, because although she'd been freed from her cage, her emotions were still locked up. They needed to be healed from all the damage she had experienced. So God used a man who believed in the power of unconditional love and non-retaliation.

Grace's first year of marriage was difficult. She didn't understand true love as she had so little of it growing up, so she fought against it, perhaps to prove her unworthiness in her own mind. Her dear friend from her teen years encouraged her to stay in the marriage. And when she acted out her dysfunction, her husband would love her rather than fight back. He told her he was in this for the long haul. His unfailing love and loyalty helped her grow and change.

Grace would tell you that if her husband had fought back or focused on his own hurt, their marriage would have fallen apart. But because of his close walk with Christ, he knew he was called to stand for this marriage and to love her unconditionally. Years later Grace's eyes still flood with tears when she speaks of her husband's steady love and her healing from the cage. Her daughters are happy and healthy, and her marriage is solid.

Just as Grace's love rescued Tasha the cat and gave her a new and better life, so Jesus' love saved Grace, not just from sin but also from her destructive past. The love of Jesus has amazing powers to free and to heal for all who are willing to receive it and give their lives to Him.

If the Son sets you free, you will be free indeed (John 8:36).

CONSIDER THIS

Have you ever been trapped in a cage from which you needed to be freed? What locked you in? What let you out? How might God use your love to release someone else?

All Shook Up

God Understands Our Weakness

I want to know God's thoughts…
the rest are details.

Albert Einstein

It was 4:31 a.m., January 17, 1994. Both my husband and I were jolted awake as our house began to shake. Having grown up in earthquake country, I was used to a little rock 'n' roll that would end before I could get overly concerned. But what awakened us on that morning was a completely different breed of temblor.

Just when all my earthquake experience made me think it would soon be over, the shaking intensified. Now the house didn't rock or roll; it pulsated sharply, as if some malicious giant were bouncing it up and down on a huge mattress. I grabbed Phil in utter terror as he was reaching for me. We weren't the only ones affected. Tiger, our adorable female gray tabby cat, had already bolted.

Normally, Tiger couldn't be pried from her spot on the bed between us. Not this night. She fled the scene before the vertical motion even occurred. Phil and I clung to each other and cried out to God for help. It was so noisy we weren't even able to hear our 14-year-old daughter Sarah screaming 30 feet away in her own bedroom. Our son Matthew tried to go to her, but he couldn't because he was being tossed around so much himself.

The first reports indicated the quake felt even bigger than it was—and it was big enough. Our house fared well. The only damage was a few cracks, some dropped plaster, and some toppled bookcases and pictures in the upstairs hall. Far worse were the aftershocks, usual after a big quake but disconcerting nonetheless. They seemed far too frequent, and each one rattled our nerves.

Perhaps that was why we didn't realize right away that Tiger had vanished. When we finally missed her, we searched for an hour before we found her. She was huddled under the sofa, peering out at me with a look of terror. We dragged her out against her will and took her outside so she could relieve herself. Then we brought her back inside, gave her food and water, and tried to comfort her. As soon as she'd eaten, she dove right back under the sofa again.

Thus began a nightly routine that continued for months. We'd pull Tiger out from under the sofa and carry her upstairs to bed with us. As soon as we set her on the mattress and let go, she'd race downstairs and hide under the sofa again. In her mind, that was the place of safety.

Tiger was having her own brand of aftershocks—aftershocks of fear. She wasn't the only one. So was I. Out of all the cats and humans in our house, we alone continued to be traumatized. I expended a lot of energy anticipating the next jolt. I dressed very quickly. I kept my shoes on at all times, in case I needed to run. I dreaded being home alone. I wouldn't go to bed without Phil, so I slept on the sofa each night until he was ready to go upstairs.

I wrestled with self-condemnation along with fear. I was co-teaching a Bible study class and began to wonder if I should continue. Shouldn't a Bible teacher be able to get the victory over a traumatic event? Shouldn't she be able to apply the verses she knew and loved about God's sovereignty? I had no victory whatsoever. I felt only defeat because I lived in fear of the next aftershock. And the more I beat on myself, the more discouraged I became.

It wasn't that I ignored the Lord. I didn't. I clung to Him, begging Him to take these feelings away. I memorized Scripture. I asked my friends to pray. But nothing made a difference. I felt like a total failure in my faith.

Later I learned that this quake had many more aftershocks than normal—100 in the first week. It was an interesting fact, but even if I had known it then, it wouldn't have made me feel any better. No matter the situation, shouldn't I be able to be stronger than this—in the Lord?

But I wasn't strong. I was just like Tiger emotionally. Had I been a cat, I would have joined her under the sofa. Instead, I tried to go about my normal life, but I was jumpy and jittery and unhappy. I believed I was a huge disappointment to the Lord. I imagined that He was irritated with my lack of faith. Added to my fear of aftershocks was the fear that God was frowning at me.

Then, one day God used Tiger to speak to me. I was sitting on the sofa and studying the Bible when she wiggled her way out from under and sat down. My heart was gladdened when she came out of her own volition, and I wanted to give her comfort. I laid my Bible aside and moved to the edge of the sofa to pet and talk to her. "Poor little Tiger," I soothed. "I'm so sorry you're having such a hard time right now. I love you so much. You are my special little cat. Eventually things will return to normal."

In my heart I heard the Lord speak to me. It was as if He said, "Dottie, you are my Tiger." My heart leaped. He wasn't condemning me after all. He still loved me in my distress, and He wanted me to know that.

I felt suddenly free again—not from aftershocks, but from the disapproval I had been ascribing to the Lord. I realized these feelings had been self-imposed and I had been too hard on myself. God met me where I was, hiding under the sofa in my heart, to comfort and encourage me.

Tiger and I eventually got over our terror and went back to life as usual. But I learned a valuable lesson. As God's child, I am loved!

Regardless of how hard I am on myself, God loves me. Regardless of whether I'm brave or fearful, His love can reach me.

I learned that nothing can separate me from the love of God which is in Christ Jesus—not even an earthquake!

As a father has compassion on his children, so the Lord has compassion on those who fear him; for he knows how we are formed, he remembers that we are dust (Psalm 103:13-14).

CONSIDER THIS

Have you ever hidden under the sofa of life because of a trauma you suffered? Did you think God condemned you? Did you condemn yourself? How did God meet you where you were and show you love and compassion? How might you do this for others?

Nine Lives and Life Eternal

Christ Conquered Death

Death—the last sleep? No, it
is the final awakening.

Sir Walter Scott

If cats have nine lives, as the saying goes, then Merlin had already used up at least one by the time I got him. He'd collided with a car and lived to meow the tale. He might have used up an additional life when he took a flying leap in my kitchen. He missed, but landed none the worse for his stunt. Though it isn't likely this could have proved fatal for an agile feline, let's tick off life number two, just for argument's sake. That still left seven. And seven lives, or even one or two shy of that, should have kept him going anywhere from ten to fifteen years or more.

He lived for not quite six.

A temporary housemate of mine was the first to notice something was wrong. Merlin was a special favorite of hers. She told me she thought he was losing weight. He seemed clingy too, wrapping his paws around her neck when she held him. Then he started markedly favoring one of his legs. I noticed a swelling. I wondered if Merlin had scuffled with another of my cats. Perhaps he had an infected scratch or bite. I whisked him off to the vet, who suspected the same and put him on antibiotics.

To my consternation, Merlin had a horrible reaction to the medication. He couldn't keep food down. The vet said to bring him right back. A second exam raised a far more serious concern. The swelling might be not an abscess, but a tumor.

Test results confirmed this. Merlin had an aggressive form of cancer. They could take off his leg and do radiation or chemo, but there was no guarantee such measures would save him. It was possible the cancer had already spread.

Given such odds, how much do you put an animal through? It wasn't an easy decision. I talked to friends, agonized, and prayed. Ultimately, I took him to a homeopathic vet, who gave him some palliative treatment. That treatment was designed to prolong his good days and ease his passing. I took him back home, fed him lots of tuna, and watched for signs it was time to put him down. When they came, I said my farewells, took him back to the vet, and held him while he fell peacefully asleep.

Merlin's premature passing reminded me of life's unpredictability. But at least I had several weeks to prepare. I had no time at all when I lost my best friend some years before, just two days after Merlin came to live with me.

I'd been friends with Mandy for 22 years. She was the sister I never had. We'd shared countless joys and sorrows, and we both loved the Lord. But her kids were teens, and we both had busy lives. It had been six weeks since we'd last spoken with each other. And so, the Monday after Thanksgiving, I phoned and left a message on her answering machine. She called me back the next morning.

I told Mandy all about my new orange tabby, Merlin, and some little speed bumps in his adjustment. She was a cat person too and reassured me. Then she shared what a lovely Thanksgiving she'd had with her extended family. She also mentioned that her newspaper had gotten wet and she'd strung up a clothesline indoors and hung it out to dry. I wondered why she didn't just buy a new one, but she said she wanted to see if her strategy would work. That was just like Mandy…curious and creative to the core. I'm sure I was smiling inside when we said our goodbyes.

I had my Bible study class that night. Afterward, I grabbed a late dinner. It was past 10 p.m. when I finally got home. The message light was blinking on my phone. A voice I didn't recognize said to call Mandy's family…no matter what the hour.

My blood ran cold. I sensed instantly that something was terribly wrong. I dialed. Mandy's husband came on the line. Voice breaking, he told me she'd passed away. She'd taken ill suddenly. She'd been rushed to the hospital, but the doctors couldn't save her. It was either a heart attack or a stroke. She was only 50 years old.

Mandy and Merlin died prematurely, but none of us survive this life. Their loss reminds me of my own mortality. Even as a small child, I was very aware of this. I dreaded turning even one year older because I'd be a year closer to death. That fear didn't leave me when I asked Jesus into my heart. My Bible said Jesus conquered death when He died for our sins on the cross. It said that through faith in Him, I had life eternal. It said that when it came time to leave this earth I would pass into God's presence. Still, my fear remained. Did that mean my faith was somehow deficient? Friends tried to reassure me, but I wrestled with the matter. And then one year in Bible study, God gave me a whole new perspective on death and how it might actually reflect His love and mercy.

We were studying the book of 1 Corinthians. I don't recall the lecture, but it must have pertained to death somehow. I'd long marveled at how God gives us pictures of spiritual truths in the physical realm. Now I suddenly realized that death was such a picture. The worst part of death for those who remain is the pain of separation—of losing a loved one like Mandy or Merlin. Yet this is but a foretaste of the far greater pain of eternal separation from God. As such, it can warn us and prod us to trust Christ before it is too late.

Merlin lives on in photographs and in the hearts of those who loved him. So does Mandy…but she also lives on in the presence of God. Even if she'd been a cat, nine lives could not have saved her. But one Life did—one poured out for her on Calvary. That same Life saved me. And whether or not I fear death, it can't hold me captive. When I leave this world I'll slip through death's chains and join Mandy at God's throne of grace forever.

I will ransom them from the power of the grave; I will redeem them from death. Where, O death, are your plagues? Where, O grave, is your destruction? (Hosea 13:14).

CONSIDER THIS

What about death do you find most painful? Most frightening? Most comforting? Has your faith in God, or lack of it, influenced this? How?

Boundless Love

When We Can't Be There, God Is

May the road rise up to meet you.
May the wind always be at your back.
May the sun shine warm upon your face,
and rains fall soft upon your fields.
And until we meet again,
May God hold you in the palm of His hand.

IRISH BLESSING

Kitty would have been good with a cell phone. She always wanted to know where we were and what we were doing. She followed us all over our 120 acres of farmland. It was clear that Kitty had a purpose and a goal. She wanted to be near us at all times.

But Kitty had her own fixed boundaries beyond which she would not go. One of these was the almond orchard. Our daughter Karen sometimes would walk the two and a half miles to her grandparents' home. Kitty followed her to the end of the orchard. Karen knelt down to pet her and talk to her. Then she waved goodbye and walked on, but she kept looking back to find out if Kitty was still there. Kitty remained sitting where they'd parted until Karen couldn't see her any longer. When Karen returned, Kitty met her at the edge of the orchard and they went back home together.

Sometimes Kitty walked me to my car. She would follow as I slowly backed down our driveway onto the road. But she would go only to the end of the driveway, sit down, and watch me drive out of sight. This was another boundary she would not cross, much as she wished to be with me.

Steve and I also came to a boundary we could not cross to be with our loved ones. The boundary of heaven stands between us and our firstborn twins. I still miss our tiny ones in a special way. They were with us for such a short time.

Stephen Paul and Erin Rene were born prematurely in early May 1976. They were both very tiny, one pound three ounces and one pound four ounces, respectively. If this had happened today, with all the medical advances that have taken place, they might have had a better chance. But they were born more than 30 years ago.

Stephen gave up after just a few hours, but Erin seemed to fight for life. My doctor told me that if she lived they would take her to a special neonatal hospital. I was exhausted from three days of labor. My doctor said to rest. My husband, who was also spent, went home to sleep, and my brother, Darrell, stayed in the hospital with me.

Early the next morning I woke up suddenly, knowing I had to be near Erin. I went to the nursery and stood by her little incubator. She was working so hard to breathe. She had no fat on her tiny body, so I could even see her heart beating. I wanted so badly to help her, but there was nothing I could do.

A nurse came over and gently told me we could take Erin out of her incubator and I could hold her because she didn't have long to live. She carefully lifted my precious baby and laid her in my arms. She asked if she could get me anything. I said yes, I would like my brother to be near. She knew where he was and quickly left to bring him.

Darrell stood on the other side of the large glass nursery window while I talked to Erin about how I'd thought we would spend our lives together. I told her about her home, her room, her daddy. I talked about her first tooth, her first step, and her first birthday. I told her about her first day of school and her high school graduation. I spoke of how happy her daddy and I were that she'd been born and how I'd already prayed for her husband. As I talked I prayed, and I watched her tired little body breathe more and more slowly. Her heartbeat was also slowing. As I held her and stroked her soft skin, my tears fell on her.

I knew Darrell longed to stand close beside me, to help me through this pain. But he wasn't allowed to enter the nursery. All he could do was stand behind the window and pray. His physical boundary was the glass. But his prayers knew no boundaries—and God didn't, either.

Putting a whole lifetime of caring for my child into these few short hours was one of the most powerful experiences of my life. When I fell silent at last and just calmly held her, I felt Jesus right there with us. Finally her breathing stopped, her heart stopped, and I could feel her spirit lift from her little body. Just like her brother, she went from my arms to His.

Kitty's boundary was the orchard. She couldn't go to Grandma and Grandpa's with Karen. But God was with Karen all the way.

Darrell's boundary was the big glass window that separated him from Erin and me. He couldn't cross it. But his prayers could—and God was with us too.

The boundary between Erin and me was the door to eternal life. It wasn't my time to walk through, so Jesus took her. He has no boundaries and His love knows no limits. Steve and I will see our twins again because we have forgiveness of sins and eternal life through Jesus, God's Son. One day we will cross the boundary of this world, and the door of heaven will open for us, just as it did for them.

Where can I go from your Spirit? Where can I flee from your presence? If I go up to the heavens, you are there; if I make my bed in the depths, you are there. If I rise on the wings of the dawn, if I settle on the far side of the sea, even there your hand will guide me, your right hand will hold me fast (Psalm 139:7-10).

Consider This

Do you have loved ones you wish you could be with who are separated from you? What about this is most difficult to deal with? How do you pray for them? Have you seen evidences of God's love and protection in their lives? How has this comforted you?

Twilight Cats

Be Faithful, As God Is

Let love and faithfulness never leave you; bind them around your neck, write them on the tablet of your heart.

PROVERBS 3:3

Barney and Misty are "twilight cats." They are nearing the end of their lives. Barney turns 19 this year, and Misty turns 18. The four-foots I brought home as kittens have become an "old man" and "old woman"—and their age has really been showing.

Barney's limbs have stiffened. When he was younger, he could spring from the kitchen counter to the top of a high cabinet above my oven. From that penthouse perch he'd survey his world or curl up for a snooze. Now even the counter is far beyond his reach, and his gait is wooden when he climbs the stairs. I once put the cats' food high up out of dogs' reach, but I've had to relocate their dishes so Barney can get to his dinner.

Always a talker, Barney has taken to yowling incessantly at times. The vet says one cause may be kitty senility. In contrast, Misty plays "silent senior" to Barney's aging vocalizations. She'll go off and curl up by herself, easy to forget and neglect, the way some elderly humans are.

Both cats have beginning kidney failure and must be on special food. They don't groom themselves as well as they used to, either. And Barney's bathroom habits, never stellar, have grown worse.

In short, growing older isn't always pretty. Recently I confessed to a friend that I don't like dealing with the messier aspects of aging. I'm ashamed of it, but it's true—not just of my feline family, but my human one also.

Mom is 90 now. The woman who once went three days a week to a gym now needs help to pull herself out of a chair. If she walks any distance, she holds someone's arm for support. She's had chronic leukemia for years, and it's taken a toll on her body, even though her mind remains sharp. She hates her loss of mobility and independence. Recently she told me she wished she could take care of simple needs without a big fuss. Just tending to her health and everyday tasks takes huge time and effort.

Because Mom has money to hire caregivers, I'm not involved in her daily care. I've been spared the messier aspects of her aging… most of the time. That's not true of my friend and prayer partner, Lee. Some time ago he felt God's call to move back to his mother's home so he could care for her.

Lee's mom was living on her own, but she had some major health challenges. Not long after Lee moved in, her health worsened. Over the past couple of years she's been hospitalized multiple times, had nursing home stays, and required constant monitoring at home. Through it all Lee has functioned as his mother's primary caregiver and support. He has overseen her medications, taken her to medical appointments, and functioned as a go-between with a host of doctors and therapists. He has been her cheerleader and her advocate. He has fought to keep her from giving up, and he has pursued every possibility to improve her health and quality of life.

Lee and I live in different states, but we talk once a week on the phone. Some weeks he sounds encouraged. Others find him hurting and burned out. But, no matter how tired or discouraged or stressed he feels, he never wavers in his faithfulness. He never questions God's call to be there for his mom, even when it's tough. He's talked about needing a break, but not of quitting. He is determined to do what God wants and be there for the parent who needs him, even when the going gets rough.

Lee and his mother have trusted Christ as their personal Lord and Savior. He leans on God for help. He prays for strength and wisdom. He finds comfort and encouragement in the prayers of caring friends. When I asked him if I could tell his story, he said the one thing he'd want to share with others in his situation is the helpfulness of spiritual support. Lee makes it a point to take advantage of available spiritual resources. When his mom has been hospitalized, he's sought out the hospital chaplain. There have been moments when Lee wasn't there that the chaplain stopped by to visit his mom and was able to encourage her.

As I write this, Lee's mother is back in a skilled care facility yet again. He's not sure how long she will be here on this earth. I don't know how long I'll have my own mom—or Barney and Misty, either. But I do know that God wants me to be faithful to the elderly in my life, be they pets or people. I know this because Jesus said, "So in everything, do to others what you would have them do to you" (Matthew 7:12).

Truth be told, if I live long enough, someday I'll be old and messy too. Maybe that's why I find it tough to deal with twilight cats and people. Their plight is a peek at my possible future, a foretaste of what I may face someday. But it's also a reminder that through it all, God is faithful.

God won't desert me when I become old or difficult to deal with. If anything, He'll draw closer than ever when my earthly shell starts to break down. And one day, when I leave this life, He will welcome me into His presence to enjoy a breakdown-free eternity with Him.

Rise in the presence of the aged, show respect for the elderly and revere your God. I am the LORD (Leviticus 19:32).

CONSIDER THIS

What are some ways that people have been faithful to you in your life? What are some ways God has been faithful? Are there elderly people you might be faithful to? How?

Uno, Dos, Grace

God Sustains the Lonely

Loneliness is the first thing which
God's eye named, not good.

John Milton

I was the youngest of five children. When I was about nine years old, my sisters were all grown up, my brother, Darrell, was a teenager, and I was lonely. I begged my parents for a kitten. Family friends had a litter that was ready to give away, so my parents told me I could pick one for my very own.

Mom took me over to see the kittens. There were only two left. They looked exactly alike. They were black with white paws. Mom's friend said I could hold one if I wanted to. But there was a problem. How could I choose? What would be worse, how could I leave one behind?

My overwhelming excitement and happiness quickly turned to sadness. My head dropped. Tears spilled from my face. Mom's friend was confused. She asked what was wrong. She'd thought I would love these kittens.

Mom knew right away what was bothering me. She laid a hand on my shoulder. "Oh, she does love them," Mom told her friend. "But there are only two kittens. If she took one, the other would be left alone. So if it's all right, I think we would like to take both. What do you think, Connie?"

I thought that would be great, so we took both kittens home. I brought them into our house and showed them around. I laid them on a comfy blanket in my bedroom. They walked around a bit, settled down, and went to sleep. I felt like a real mom.

I was happy, but I think Mom was worried about how Dad would respond. When he came home for lunch he asked to see the kitten. Mom started to explain how one became two while I nervously retrieved them.

Dad put the tiny creatures on his lap. He actually seemed to like them. "So what are you gonna call 'em?" he asked.

"I don't know," I replied.

"Uno and Dos," he declared. "That means one and two in Spanish."

I was thrilled. "I love it! Thank you, Dad. Hi, Uno and Dos."

Uno and Dos were my responsibility. I fed them and took care of all their other needs. I held them and petted them and even read them stories. I took them outside, and they played in the dirt beside me. They also did a real kitty thing—they climbed our big shade tree. I liked climbing the tree too, so we all sat up there together and had good long talks.

When I went to school I had to leave Uno and Dos outside. It was all right, though, because they had each other. They climbed the tree and sat on its limbs, napped on the lawn, and played tag with each other. I knew they were happy, so I didn't mind not being with them.

One day when I got home after school, my mom sat me down and told me that something very sad had happened while I was gone. She'd been cleaning the kitchen and looked out the window just in time to see one of the kittens fall from the tree. It had climbed to a high branch, so when it fell it was killed instantly. I started to bawl. Mom had tears in her eyes too.

"Who died, and where is the other one?" I sobbed.

She said she couldn't tell them apart, but she had put the surviving kitten in my room. I raced through the door and there lay Uno, sleeping on his blanket, all alone. I picked him up. As I held him, I kept crying. It seemed that he was crying too.

This took place on a Friday, so I was able to spend all of Saturday with Uno. He didn't want to do much. He just wanted me to hold him. For the rest of his life, Uno seemed sad. He didn't want to play. He didn't eat much. He just roamed the house or yard looking lonely as could be.

Seeing Uno so sad and alone was horrible for all of us. Everyone tried to cheer him up, but no one could do anything that made him even a little better. The vet said Uno was so lonely for Dos that he was giving up on life. One morning I got up to care for him, only to find that he'd passed away during the night.

When Dos died, it was as though a part of Uno went with him. Though we can't draw exact parallels between animal and human loss, this made me reflect on what happens when someone loses their spouse. When one partner dies, the other often has a hard time adjusting. My dad died when my mom was only 56 years old. They'd loved being with each other. They'd worked together, they'd worshipped together, they'd traveled together.

Mom was so young to be left alone. All five of her children were married and busy with their own lives. Mom didn't want to go on living, but she knew she must. She believed God had left her here on this earth for a reason, and she had to find it. It wasn't easy, but she pushed herself back into the world to serve Him, and He gave her grace to do so. She cooked for two organizations in our hometown. She worked as a volunteer at the retirement home. She went to Bible study. And most importantly, she prayed.

Mom is a prayer warrior. When Dad died there were 25 of us in our family. Now there are 60. We have all depended on the prayers of our mother, through birth and death, health problems, work problems—any problems. She has also taught us to pray. When there is a need, our family is on the phone or on e-mail, sharing prayer concerns and praises. Prayer has held us together, and Mom has taken the lead.

If Mom had decided to give up when Dad died, the way Uno gave up when Dos died, sorrow would have overcome her life. But she allowed God to comfort and guide her. God honored her obedience, was with her in her loneliness, and grew and blessed her even as she blessed us.

A father to the fatherless, a defender of widows, is God in his holy dwelling (Psalm 68:5).

CONSIDER THIS

Have people in your circle of family or friends lost a spouse? What was hardest for them? What helped them the most? How might you be used of God to help comfort and encourage them in their loneliness?

Part II

Stretching Exercises

God Stimulates Our Growth

MIDNIGHT

Don't Let the Birds Get to You

Trust God's Sovereignty

Before me, even as behind,
God is, and all is well.

John Greenleaf Whittier

Spring is a special time of the year. I love watching my roses come to life again as the days grow longer. The air smells wonderful with the change from winter to spring. And Midnight changes from lying in a sunspot on the rug to lying in the sunlight in the yard. Usually she can hardly wait for me to open the door. She rushes out and finds just the right place to sunbathe. Not this spring, however. She had met her match with the blue jays.

It was as if those birds had declared war on our poor cat. Each time she went outside they came in tandem to dive-bomb and peck at her, chasing her out of her usual spots. One day she took refuge under the house. Another day she fled into the garage. They were bold enough to follow her there, jumping all about as they squawked, terrorizing her. My husband and I had to go and chase them out. This kind of thing went on for more than a week. Finally, it seemed the birds had won the battle. Midnight didn't even try to go out anymore. Instead, she found places in the house to curl up. At first it was any sunspot. But the blue jays would perch where they could see her and keep squawking at her. Finally she searched out places where she couldn't be seen, so she could sleep in peace.

I watched in sadness as Midnight fled from these birds. They had changed her life. What had happened to my bold little hunter cat? Years before we'd had a beautiful tortoiseshell cat who was also harassed by two blue jays, but she refused to be intimidated. She would either roll around and bat at them as they came at her or ignore them completely. When she finally caught one, we actually cheered her victory. That's how annoying the blue jays had become, and that was the reason we hated how quickly Midnight gave up. We wanted her to stand her ground with the bothersome birds. Alas, that was not the reality in our home. Midnight just ate and went to hide. It was a quiet house full of defeat.

And then one day I was writing a lecture for the Bible study class I teach when I heard a great commotion of squawking. The sound was so loud I thought the birds must be inside my bedroom, so I got up to investigate. The sight that greeted me was so remarkable that I grabbed my camera and took a photo. Midnight was on the back of a cushioned chair and the birds were only about a foot away, yet she sat serene and unconcerned. What made the difference was the glass French door that separated her from them. Midnight understood that she was safe behind the glass. I think she must have decided "enough is enough" to be curled up in clear sight of them. She refused to let the birds rule her life anymore. The birds were hopping and squawking, thinking they would bully her and win once more, but that didn't happen this time.

It occurred to me as I watched Midnight that we all have "birds" that try to peck at us, scare us, and intimidate us. The Bible says we are in a war and we need to stand firm against the enemy. We are not to let the birds get to us, and when they do, God wants us to take our stand, knowing His sovereign plan is the glass that protects us.

My dear friend Jean found herself hiding from the "birds" following the terrorist attacks of September 11, 2001. Jean is a songwriter, worship leader, and guitar teacher. She, like the rest of us in America, was deeply distressed on the day we now call 9-11. She was worried that the terrorists would hit Los Angeles next. This was her beloved city, and she was consumed with fear. I think most of us watched our televisions more than usual during that period, but Jean couldn't stop. She had the TV on every waking moment. When she had to go out on an errand, she was glued to news on the car radio. She continued to monitor the news for any new attacks. She was unsettled, and her state of mind made her miserable and joyless.

It wasn't like Jean to feel overwhelmed like this. Normally, peace rules her life. She has a childlike faith most of us long for. Jean is a person who walks closely with God and is deeply aware of His presence. She sees the Lord in every moment, and she feels a close communion with Him, especially while writing and singing her praise songs. But not in this instance. She was like Midnight, hiding from the birds and living in misery.

Jean had been robbed of the sweet fellowship she normally shared with the Lord. This went on for weeks. Then one day she realized the terrorist attacks were no surprise to God. He was still sovereign—and His sovereignty stood between her and the evil she feared, just as the glass French door stood between Midnight and those blue jays. Jean resolved not to let fear rule her life and steal her peace anymore. That very day she picked up her guitar and began to sing to the Lord. A new song came to her, about how God knows everything and has a plan that nothing and no one can reverse. She called it "His Plan."

Jean had begun to take her stand again. No longer was she intimidated by the evil in this world. She was resting in the fact that God was in control. His sovereign plan would be carried out no matter what. She also decided that even if the terrorists took her life, she was still safe in God's hands for eternity.

Midnight only felt safe enough to start living a more normal life again after she realized our glass door protected her. For Jean it was remembering and relying on God's sovereignty. If your "birds" are getting to you, remind yourself that God's in control, take your stand, and put your trust in Him.

Praise be to the name of God for ever and ever; wisdom and power are his...He reveals deep and hidden things; he knows what lies in darkness, and light dwells with him (Daniel 2:20,22).

CONSIDER THIS

Do you have birds that are getting to you and robbing you of your peace? What about them frightens you? How is this affecting your life? How might the awareness of God's sovereignty change your perspective and free you?

Grease

Dare to Share Your Faith

Nothing will ever be attempted if all possible objections must first be overcome.

Samuel Johnson

Lucy was a cat who always brought us challenges. When we first got him, we thought he was a docile female kitten. It didn't take us long to realize that "she" was a "he." Nor was Lucy mellow. He could be downright mean, even to those who loved and cared for him. He would attack our daughter Karen when she stopped petting him sooner than he wanted. He'd bite our son, John, while he worked on his truck. We all had our own stories about Lucy—and the scars to prove them.

One day Lucy showed up totally covered in auto grease. He looked horrible, and it was obvious he was miserable. John and Karen realized Lucy would get sick if he tried to lick himself clean, so they decided to risk bathing him. They figured this would likely be troublesome, so they armed themselves for danger. They put on old pants, heavy sweatshirts with hoods, old shoes, and thick rubber gloves. Karen got the bath water ready while John attempted to pick up our huge, greasy, unhappy cat.

Lucy must have realized his problem because he actually let John hold him. Tension rose as John carried him into the bathroom. As he lowered Lucy into the tub, we had high expectations that he would leap out, attack John and Karen, and flee. But, to everyone's surprise, none of that took place. Lucy actually calmed down in the water and allowed them to wash and rewash him until he was completely grease free.

Lucy never would have gotten clean if John and Karen hadn't been willing to dress themselves for battle and take a risk. God calls His children to take a risk too, and dress in His armor to share His truth with those who are covered with the spiritual grease of sin.

Not long ago I ran into a lifelong friend. We were both at the hospital visiting patients. I'd once thought my friend had given his life to Jesus as a boy. But I was no longer so sure because he had embraced the belief that there are many ways to God. In his journey through life, he'd picked up a lot of grease. It weighed him down and blurred the truth. I knew I needed to talk with him about this.

Just as John and Karen had dressed themselves in protective clothing, I put on the full armor of God. I clothed myself with the belt of truth and the breastplate of righteousness. I prayed for peace. I had the shield of faith that God was helping me. I wore the helmet of salvation, and I asked God's Spirit to be my sword and bring the Scriptures I needed to my mind.

I reminded my friend that Jesus said, "I am the way and the truth and the life. No one comes to the Father except through me" (John 14:6). I prayed for the right words as we talked about this. I was hoping he would welcome a chance to be bathed, as Lucy had. But although he didn't attack me, he didn't see his need for cleansing. He didn't agree that "all have sinned and fall short of the glory of God" (Romans 3:23). He thought he was a good man and didn't need a Savior.

When we parted, we hugged, but it saddened me to know he

was drowning in the grease of this life and refusing help. I could have felt that I'd failed, but I didn't. I had done what I could. He was the one who had to choose to be cleansed or not. And unlike Lucy, he hadn't seen his need.

Many of the Pharisees in Jesus' day didn't see their need, either. Because they looked clean on the outside, they thought they were fine. Jesus called them "whitewashed sepulchers" and warned they were coated with grease on the inside, but they rejected Him. Not so the publicans and sinners He shared with who were coated in outer grease, like Lucy. Many saw their need and trusted in the Lord. They let themselves be washed in His blood and were left clean and comfortable, just as our cat was.

God calls us to share the truth of the gospel, but He warns us that not all will receive our message. Some, like Lucy, may be eager for cleansing. Others, like my friend, may seem to reject it. But we don't know what ongoing effect our words may have. It is God who degreases. It's His Spirit who works on hearts. God promises His Word won't come back to Him void. Our part is simply to obey, share His truth, and leave the results to Him.

You will receive power when the Holy Spirit comes on you; and you will be my witnesses in Jerusalem, and in all Judea and Samaria, and to the ends of the earth (Acts 1:8).

CONSIDER THIS

Have you ever shared the gospel with others? If not, what is keeping you from it? If so, what about it do you find most daunting? What do you find most exciting? What do you find most encouraging?

Have you ever had someone reject the message and later come to faith in Christ? How did it happen, and how did it make you feel?

Bold is Beautiful

God Wants Us to Pray

A prayer in its simplest definition is
merely a wish turned Godward.

PHILLIPS BROOKS

There it was again! Another howl from Midnight woke me out of a deep sleep. It was a hot summer night that already seemed much longer than any night should be. All I wanted to do was sleep soundly, but every time I reached that point she would yowl beneath my open window. She knew exactly where I was, and she knew she could wake me.

This time I decided I'd better not go back to sleep until I had settled the matter, so I dragged myself up, plodded down the stairs and let her in. She rubbed my leg on her way to her food dish. After a couple of bites of kibble, she went back to the door to be let out again, and I gladly complied.

As I wearily made my way upstairs to bed, I noted it was 3 a.m. The howling had begun before midnight. As I drifted off to sleep I thought about a parable Jesus had told. There was a friend who came to ask for some bread in the night. Wasn't that at midnight as well?

I finally finished my night's sleep in peace. The next morning I looked up the parable in Luke 11. Sure enough, it happened at midnight. One friend asked the other to lend him three loaves of bread, and the one sleeping said, "Don't bother me."

Jesus said, in verse 8, "Though he will not get up and give him the bread because he is his friend, yet because of the man's boldness he will get up and give him as much as he needs."

Jesus was teaching His disciples about prayer through a parable. The primary point of this one is the need for boldness in prayer. Jesus continued in verse 9, "So I say to you: Ask and it will be given to you; seek and you will find; knock and the door will be opened to you."

Midnight got what she wanted from me, not because of my love for her, although I do love her very much, but because of her persistent howling. She was bold!

I have been howling to God for nearly three years now on behalf of my dear friend Linda, who has been afflicted with fibromyalgia, a chronic disorder characterized by widespread pain. Linda and I have been in a prayer group for more than 20 years with two other close friends, Peggy and Karen. We've prayed each other through hard times, joyous times, illnesses, sins, financial struggles, and family struggles. You name it and we've probably prayed for it.

Over the years we've taken prayer requests from each others' children and families as seriously as we have those from our own. Peggy recently signed a card from us to a new member of her family with "from your prayer-in-laws." We still try to meet each week to come in our weakness to the throne of God, but these days we are missing Linda.

Three years ago we saw Linda's health begin to fail. As her pain escalated, her world shrank. She began to drop commitments and activities because the pain would intensify each time she pushed herself to go. We moved our prayer meeting to her house to help her. She saw specialist after specialist and tried program after program. We prayed constantly for her to be healed. We also decided we would not behave in the way Job's friends had. They believed Job had done something to offend God, and his suffering was the result. They told him this and added to his anguish. Karen said, "Job's friends thought they had all the answers, but we're in a better position than they. We understand that we know nothing!" But we did know how to pray, and pray we did.

We intensified our prayers, we laid hands on Linda, we worshipped God, we took communion, and we watched in helplessness as her condition worsened. Through this period of time, Linda's faith was amazing. Even though she could neither read her Bible nor go to church or Bible studies, she knew God was with her. She learned not to use the word "why." Instead she talked about how He would use it all.

Then she hit a period of pain so intense she felt as if she were entering the dark night of her soul. She lost all hope and felt only despair. During those dark days we continued to howl to God just as Midnight had done that one night. We thanked Him for hearing us, we praised Him for who He is, we confessed our confusion, and we continued to go "boldly to the throne of grace" (Hebrews 4:16 NKJV).

Linda's condition didn't improve immediately, but slowly we noticed that she was able to do a little more. She began eating better. She began to move more because the intense, burning pain let up enough for her to do so. And she began to have hope again.

Today Linda is still quite ill, but she is somewhat better than at her lowest point. I asked her why she thought she was better, and she said it was because God was answering all those prayers. She also said that she's not out of the woods yet, but she's out of the coffin!

We will continue to howl to heaven for Linda's well-being because we love her and miss her—but more than that, because we are doing what Jesus told us to do. He urged boldness in prayer.

Through this 20-year journey in prayer, there is one thing we have discovered: Prayer is essential! It's as vital as an oxygen tank at the bottom of the sea. We won't know the answers to any of the why questions this side of heaven, but that mustn't stop us from howling at God's window.

What a remarkable privilege not only to be allowed to come to the throne of God in prayer, but also to be encouraged to come boldly.

Midnight got what she wanted, not because of my love for her, but because of her boldness in howling. How much more will our gracious God respond to His children's bold prayers after He told us to ask, seek, and knock.

Epaphras, who is one of you and a servant of Christ Jesus, sends greetings. He is always wrestling in prayer for you (Colossians 4:12).

CONSIDER THIS

What about prayer do you find most exciting? What do you find most puzzling? Do you have prayers that have seemed to go unanswered? If so, are you still howling to God about these requests? Why or why not?

The Treat Not Taken

Taste All of God's Goodness

God's gifts put man's best dreams to shame.

Elizabeth Barrett Browning

I set out the yummy new delicacy beside the kitties' normal meal. Which would they take, prime choice select barbecued tri-tip steak or sale-priced cat food? I wanted to treat them to something special. I was also curious to see if they would sample a food they had never tasted before.

Our kitties eat cat food all the time. They also catch rodents and birds. They scrounge through the garbage can for scraps. But I was offering them a savory piece of meat Steve had cooked. Steve is known for his barbecue. He uses wonderful spices and times the cooking just right. I only offered it to the cats to see what they would do. Normally I don't share this wonderful treat.

Sammy, one of the neighbor cats, was standing by the food bowl when I brought out the steak. She looked at the tri-tip and kept right on eating the cat food. Then our cat Michelin came around. She also looked at the beef and walked away. I had to guess that because these kitties had never seen this treat before, they just assumed it wouldn't be good and decided to ignore it.

I went back in, but Karen stayed outside, watching from a distance. Finally our cat Milkshake appeared. He eyed the meat. He looked at the other two felines. He saw that they didn't want it, so he gobbled it up. He wasn't afraid to try something new from his masters, so he had a wonderful treat. I'm sure he enjoyed it!

Watching those cats refuse a gift they didn't understand reminded me of how my sister Sharon once did the same thing. She lives in Nebraska. Our mom lives in my hometown of Bakersfield, California. One day Mom spotted a book she knew Sharon would love to read and have for herself. She bought a copy and mailed it to my sister.

Sharon was excited to see the package. She tore it open, only to find a book called *90 Days of Rice.* Not only was she disappointed, but she felt a little hurt that Mom would send her a diet book. She put it on a table and left it there for quite some time.

Mom never heard anything from Sharon, so after a while she called and asked if her present had been received. Sharon swallowed hard. She told Mom she was sorry she hadn't called or written to thank her. Then she confessed she'd felt a bit hurt that Mom would think a diet book was a good gift when Sharon hadn't asked for one.

Mom started laughing. She was laughing so hard that it sounded to Sharon as if she were crying. Sharon shouted over the noise that she was sorry. She would read the book now.

Mom stopped laughing, took a deep breath, and clued Sharon in. The book had nothing to do with dieting. It was a book about World War II written by Sharon's seventh grade math teacher. He'd been a prisoner of war and had only rice to eat for 90 days. The book was his autobiography.

Then Mom and Sharon had a great laugh together. Sharon had almost missed out on a wonderful gift because she was unfamiliar with the book and didn't realize what it really was.

We can also miss out on God's gifts because we're unfamiliar with them and don't realize what they are or how they can bless us. Years ago this almost happened to a friend of mine who was a new Christian. She told me that she loved to read the Bible, but she stuck to the New Testament. I asked her why. She said she figured the Old Testament would be really boring and not worth reading. She'd heard it was just filled with stuff about who begat whom.

I told her that yes, there were lots of begats, but in these begats we learned where Jesus came from. And there was so much more to read in the Old Testament. There were marvelous stories about people's faith in the Lord and how He worked with them. There was poetry and wisdom literature. And our Christian faith had its very foundations in Old Testament Scripture. Then I told her to read the Book of Esther and get back to me.

When we met again, my friend was beaming from ear to ear. "So," I said, "you must have read Esther." She said she'd not only read Esther, but Psalms and the Song of Solomon, and so much more. She was amazed at how much there was to learn in these Old Testament books. She loved the poetry of the Psalms, and how they expressed such sadness and joy. She talked about the love story in the Song of Solomon and how she couldn't wait to read it with her husband. She told me that she'd learned so much about the people of the Bible as she'd read their stories. She now saw how the Old Testament led up to the New Testament, and that its beautiful writings had so much to teach.

I'm thrilled my friend did not ignore God's marvelous gift of the Old Testament just because it felt unfamiliar and strange at first. I pray we all partake of its spiritual "meat." Through the Word we can gain wonderful insights into who God is and receive all the fullness of the knowledge and blessings He has to offer.

All Scripture is God-breathed and is useful for teaching, rebuking, correcting and training in righteousness (2 Timothy 3:16).

CONSIDER THIS

What is your favorite book of the Old Testament? Why? What has it taught you? How has it deepened your faith? Is there an Old Testament book you've never tasted that you might like to sample?

Great Expectations

Trust God to Provide

Every tomorrow has two handles. We can take hold of it with the handle of anxiety or the handle of faith.

Henry Ward Beecher

Bonco was my mom's laid-back orange tabby. This cat knew which side his kibble was buttered on. Experience taught him that his humans would supply his food. So he saw no reason to get his fur all in a dither if some of it got stolen…as it often did.

Because Bonco was an outdoor cat, he was fed on the patio Ping-Pong table. This kept ground-bound critters like Mom's dog out of his bowl. It did nothing to deter a feathered thief. Some resident blue jays decided this cat's kibble was "for the birds" and dug in their beaks.

Blue jays can be extremely aggressive. Bonco wasn't about to fight for what he fully expected would be replenished. He'd sit on a front corner of the table, watching three or four birds chow down at his bowl on the table's back end. He didn't stress. He knew there'd be more kibble where that came from, and there always was.

Well, almost always.

When it rained, the food bowl wasn't always refilled quite as quickly as normal. But that didn't shake Bonco's trust in his human providers. He didn't give up on them and go off to hunt his own dinner if his bowl was empty. He did what was normally forbidden. He marched through the dog door and into the kitchen to meow for his due. Once he got his request he went back outside where he belonged. He had faith in his humans, and his great expectations were rewarded.

My great expectations were rewarded too, when I asked God in faith to fill my creative food bowl with ideas for a novel I was writing.

I was nearing the end of the second volume in a Christian fantasy trilogy. It had been a struggle, as my writing often is. Though I felt that God had called me to the work and I asked Him for inspiration, I didn't fully trust His provision. Fear of failure met me daily at my computer, stealing my productiveness just as surely as those blue jays stole Bonco's kibble. Now it was crunch time. My ministry partners on the project were meeting with a publisher in two weeks on an unrelated matter. They hoped this publisher might take the trilogy too. They wanted to show a draft of the book I was working on. But I was a couple of chapters from done...and I hadn't exactly been speed-writing. I hoped I could do it, but my heart was in my mouth.

And then my pastor preached a sermon that cleared my spiritual vision. I realized I'd been looking to my own adequacy, not God's. I realized I needed to trust in Him to give me what I needed to do His will. I came in out of the rain of fear, marching through the door of prayer to the kitchen of God's grace to claim my spiritual dinner. I told Him I would have great expectations based not on who I was, but on who He was.

God didn't disappoint. He filled my creative food bowl to overflowing, often with ideas and connections that surprised me. I finished the book. I received notes from a member of our ministry team. I made "fixes" based on those notes in one day. As I joyfully e-mailed the manuscript, I vowed to hold close the lesson I'd learned and depend on God to provide in the future.

Yeah, right!

Imperfect human that I am, I still stumble in my faith. I'm still tempted to take my eyes off my heavenly Provider. When He sets me a task, I'm still tempted to focus on my resources rather than His. And when I do, I say, "No way"—just as Jesus' disciples did when He asked them to feed a hungry crowd who had gathered around Him (John 6:1-13).

It was getting late. Jesus' disciples asked Him to send the multitude off to find food. Jesus told the disciples to feed the crowd instead, but they didn't exactly have great expectations. They looked at the size of the task and said, "No way." Indeed, all they had was five loaves and two fishes from a little boy.

Jesus wasn't deterred. He ordered the meager fare brought to Him. He gave thanks and handed it back to the disciples to distribute. There were five thousand men, plus women and children, but everyone's food bowl got filled, and there were 12 basketfuls left over.

Bonco's human providers were faithful to meet his kitty needs for food. How much more will God faithfully supply what we need in His service? Look to His adequacy, not yours, and watch Him overflow your food bowl as you place your great expectations in Him.

My God will meet all your needs according to his glorious riches in Christ Jesus (Philippians 4:19).

CONSIDER THIS

Has God ever called you to do something you felt inadequate for? If you said yes, how did He provide? If you said no, would you make the same choice today? Why, or why not?

The Master's Call

Say Yes to God

The more we enjoy of God, the more
we are ravished with delight.

Thomas Watson

"Midnight! Midnight! Come here, baby!" That call combined with a kissing sound is how I beckon Midnight from the hill or bushes of our backyard. We first found her on our yard's wild hill about ten years ago. She was just a tiny kitten then. We guessed she had somehow wandered off from her feline family. We took her to our vet, adopted her, and kept her inside for a time to protect her.

When she grew old enough for me to let her into the backyard again, she couldn't wait to explore. Ours is a big yard for the city. I didn't want her to wander too far in her excitement and get lost. So I stayed out with her for short periods till she got used to the area, and I taught her to come when I called her.

Cats are not the easiest animals to train because they have a mind of their own. Like dogs, they want to please their masters—but only when it fits their agenda. That's why I worked so hard with

Midnight. I'm sure the neighbors got tired of hearing "Midnight, Midnight, come here, baby" over and over, but it did the job.

Whether Midnight came right away or took her time, I always gave her positive reinforcement. I'd tell her she was a good girl or I'd give her a treat. I never scolded, no matter how long it took her to respond. I wanted her to associate my call with love. And to this day, when I call her she comes, be it at a trot or a plod.

I like to think that I respond to my Master's call as faithfully as Midnight responds to me. When He first called, I was lost on my own hill of loneliness and separation. I was a teenager from a good family with a nice set of friends. I even went to church with my mom. But I didn't have a relationship with God. I didn't know I could.

Then Mom heard that a Billy Graham Crusade would be held in our area. We went the last night. The Los Angeles Coliseum was filled to the brim. It was there that I learned God calls us to believe in Jesus. Billy Graham told us that God sent His Son as the long-awaited Messiah, and those who responded to God's call and believed in Him would receive everlasting life.

This was amazing news to me. I had believed that nothing happened once a person died; that this life was all there was. It was a scary thought to me because I didn't want to go from existence to nonexistence. Now I was hearing that I could have everlasting life, and it would begin the moment I received Jesus as my Savior. Not only that, but God would forgive every bad thing I had ever done and never hold those sins against me again. If this was God's call, I wanted it! I could hardly wait to stand up, go forward, and ask Jesus into my heart. Along with many others that night, my grandmother, mother, and I responded to the call of God.

But even though I'd said yes to this call, I wasn't in a church that believed the Bible was God's Word. Our doctrinal statement looked right, but we heard things from the pulpit that contradicted what the Bible said. For example, our minister told us that Jesus was just a good man, a man of wisdom and power, who was put to death by accident. This was very different than the biblical message that Jesus was God's Son (both divine and human), and that His death was not an accident. The call I had once felt so strongly faded as I listened to wrong ideas week after week. I ended up back on the hill of loneliness and separation with all my doubts intact. I became so confused I forgot I even heard a call.

Years passed. I fell in love and was married. We bought a house and had children. When the youngest started kindergarten, I joined a Bible study class. It was part of a national ministry. A friend had invited me, and I thought, *Why not? I've studied lots of books, but never the Bible.*

It was in that class that I heard God call me for the second time. As with His first call (and all God's calls), there was a decision involved. The voice in the pulpit at my church said one thing, and the Bible I was reading said the opposite. We were studying the Gospel of Luke. It talked about the virgin birth. It claimed Jesus was the unique God-man. But my minister said the virgin birth was a myth. Which voice would I choose to believe?

Even then I sensed the decision I made would be vitally important. Now I realize that impression came from God's Spirit. This was a crucial time in my life because God was calling me to put my faith in His Word. I chose to believe the Bible over my minister—and I trotted off my lonely hill to Jesus' side. Just like Midnight, I was learning to come when my Master called me.

God had called me to trust in His Son and His Word. His third call to me was to deal with my enemy, the devil. Before I met Jesus I had dabbled in the occult. I needed to take a stand against demonic influences in my life.

I still owned a Ouija board and astrology charts. God wanted me to get rid of those items and renounce my ties with the demonic. He wanted to free me, but I had to heed His call—a call to purity, a call to follow Him only.

Just as with God's other calls, I had to make a crucial decision. I wrapped the items in a brown paper bag, threw them in the trash, and renounced my ties to my old life. I pledged my allegiance to Jesus alone.

I've had other calls in my walk with the Lord. I believe all of us have a series of calls in our life. Each involves an opportunity to respond by choosing God's way. This was certainly true of people in the Bible: Abraham, Samuel, Deborah, Esther, the disciples, and so many more. God's desire for all people is that we hear and respond to His voice; that we follow Him from that first call to faith throughout all of our days.

Midnight has learned to respond to my voice and come when I call. We can learn to respond to our Master's voice. And like Midnight, we'll find praise and blessings when we come to Him.

My sheep listen to my voice; I know them, and they follow me. I give them eternal life, and they shall never perish; no one can snatch them out of my hand (John 10:27-28).

CONSIDER THIS

What calls from God have you heard in your life? Did you trot to Him or stay on your hill? What happened as a result? If you've never responded to His call to trust Jesus, would you say yes right now?

Tabby's Mission

Press On for the Prize

Concentrate all your thoughts upon the work at hand. The sun's rays do not burn until brought to a focus.

Alexander Graham Bell

Steve, Harold, and Tabby: What a great team! When my husband, Steve, was a little boy, he and his dad loved to play with Tabby. Tabby was their wonderful kitty with a beautiful gray coat and white paws.

Tabby's favorite game was to chase a Ping-Pong ball that either Harold or Steve would bounce in the laundry room. The noise of the bouncing ball made Tabby go wild to catch it. She'd come running clear from the other end of the house and jump up and down with the ball until she could capture it in her mouth. Rather than playing fetch the way a dog would, Tabby kept knocking the ball around, chasing it from the laundry room through the kitchen and into the living room. Whether she knew it or not, she was playing "keep away" from father and son.

One day Harold and Steve decided to see just how far Tabby

would go to have the ball in her possession. When she wasn't looking, they put a chair in the doorway that separated the laundry room from the kitchen. With Steve's mom and sister watching too, Steve threw the ball into the laundry room. Tabby came rushing into the kitchen, leaped over the chair without hesitation and chased the bouncing ball back and forth from the washing machine to the back door until she caught it.

Because the chair was no problem for Tabby, her family decided to make the challenge a bit more difficult. Steve's little sister, Chrissy, brought a newspaper. They taped a sheet of it over the doorway, making sure it wasn't so high that it would be dangerous for Tabby to jump over. They let Chrissy throw the ball in this time. Tabby rushed into the kitchen, and again without any hesitation, she jumped over the paper and retrieved the bouncing ball. Parents and kids had a great laugh over this, but they weren't finished quite yet. Since Tabby had leaped this first newspaper "wall" so easily, they decided to make it a bit higher.

After they'd retaped the newspaper, Mom looked things over to make sure the new height was still safe for their kitty. At the first bounce of the Ping-Pong ball, Tabby raced around the corner from the living room. It was clear she saw the paper wall. But this time, she didn't try to jump it. To their surprise, she dove right through it—and caught the ball with just as much ease.

Everyone sat on the floor and laughed as they hugged Tabby. Then they thought about the danger Tabby could have been facing if the wall had been made of something hard. How would she know? She might have gone at it with the same intensity and been hurt. Of course, they wouldn't have let that happen. They wouldn't have even let her dive through the paper if they'd realized she'd do that (so don't try this at home, folks). But her actions were a measure of just how focused Tabby was on her task.

We have people in our family who focus like that. Our son, John, is one of them. When John decides to do something, he will think it through, lying awake at night until he has a plan. When he was finishing high school, John knew he wanted to be a mechanic because he was obviously gifted in that area. He worked on anything that came his way: tractors, pick-ups, cotton pickers, you name it. One day a family friend brought John some auto parts and told him they were the pieces of an old MG. Then he asked John to put it together. John figured out how. He was also great at diagnosing vehicle problems and was constantly asked for advice by people of all ages in our community.

John set about to decide where he would go for his mechanic's training. He investigated all the different technical trade schools. John chose a school in Arizona that met his needs most efficiently. They checked him out and gladly accepted him. When it was time, we all made the out-of-state trip to take him there and help him get settled. We helped John and his roommate find an apartment to live in. Here were two 18-year-olds right out of high school, living on their own and going to school.

For John, this was a time to work and learn. With eight hours of school and four hours of work each day, there wasn't much time left to play. After one semester, John decided he wanted to graduate sooner, so he quit his job and went to school on double sessions. He graduated several months earlier than he had first planned, and he came home to a job he'd already been offered where we live in Bakersfield.

John could have given up because of the long, hard hours, or his body could have given out. But he saw no option except to push ahead. Like Tabby, he was focused, and nothing was going to stop him.

Sadly, we are often not as focused as either Tabby or John when it comes to our spiritual lives. Paul was. He said, "For to me, to live is Christ and to die is gain" (Philippians 1:21). He pressed onward for the prize...the way Tabby did. I can only imagine what it might be like if I had the same focus on pleasing my Savior that John does on his projects and Tabby did on that Ping-Pong ball.

I have a special friend I often e-mail Scripture to. Just this morning, as I searched for a verse to send, the Lord led me to one on focus: "Know where you are headed, and you will stay on solid ground" (Proverbs 4:26 CEV). To me, that describes Tabby and John. Because they were focused, they achieved their goals. If we love and serve God with that same sense of purpose, who knows what He may accomplish in and through us for His glory.

One thing I do: Forgetting what is behind and straining toward what is ahead, I press on toward the goal to win the prize for which God has called me heavenward in Christ Jesus (Philippians 3:13-14).

CONSIDER THIS

Do you strain for the prize in your walk with the Lord? What goals might you set for yourself in this area? How might you focus in order to achieve them? How might you encourage friends or family members in their spiritual goals?

The Taming of Cats and Humans

God Grows Our Faith

Faith is different from proof; the latter is human, the former is a gift from God.

Blaise Pascal

I got my very first cats at age nine. They were feral kittens who showed up in our backyard. Taming them was a challenge, but I was up for it. I'd had turtles and lizards, but I longed for a pet with fur. My parents said not in the house, but they agreed to outdoor cats. They thought this pair might be part of a litter born under our home in a crawl space some months earlier. They had been coaxed out and then Dad secured the opening against four-footed intruders. Now these two had returned and were nosing around. But they ran from us. We had to gain their trust. We decided to woo them with food.

Our home had an outdoor brick barbecue. Flagstone steps led from it to a covered porch. We started the food bowls in front of the barbecue. As the kittens grew used to being fed, we inched their bowls closer to the porch. With time and patience, we slowly gained their confidence. At last they were eating on the porch and had become my pets.

Still these cats, whom I named Kitty and Ranger, never totally lost their wild streak. In time I was able to pet Ranger…but not Kitty. The only time I ever got to touch her was when she was nursing a litter herself and lacked the strength to flee. Even though she'd been mine for a while, her trust in me was not complete. In some areas she was still a bit skittish.

Even though I've been God's for much longer, my trust in Him is not complete, either. In some areas I'm still skittish with Him. But, as I did with those cats long ago, He keeps working with me to tame me. God uses challenges in my life to build my trust in Him—as He did with my fear of jury duty.

Being prone to guilt, I had always dreaded this particular civic duty. I feared if I got on a case, I would have an awful time. I figured I'd keep second-guessing myself about whatever decision I reached and be tortured by it for months or years to come. Though I'd learned many people have such concerns, I'd always begged God not to let me get picked to serve on an actual trial. I hadn't been. And then God convicted me to change that prayer.

Staring at my latest summons, I heard God whisper, "Shouldn't you be willing as My child to shoulder this responsibility? Won't you trust Me to provide what you need to do so?" Skittish as I felt, I knew I had to take a step of faith. And so, shaking in my spiritual boots, I told God I didn't want to serve, but I wanted His will, not mine, to be done.

I had nibbled at God's spiritual food bowl, and He took me at my word. He began to coax me down the path from the brick barbecue of fear to the covered porch of trust. He inched me closer bit by bit, just as I had done with Kitty and Ranger on that flagstone path so many years before.

Where I live, jurors are on call for a week. Each night they phone in to see if they're needed next day. If I got through the week without having to go in, I was finished.

"Please, Lord, don't let me have to report. Yet not my will, but Yours..."

I got my will the first three nights—and then I was told to report on Thursday.

Still, there was a chance I'd go free at day's end. If by that time I wasn't on a jury or on a panel from which a jury would be chosen, this personal nightmare would be over.

"Please don't let them pick me. Yet not my will..."

They picked me for a panel and chose me for the jury.

Even then I had one ray of hope left. There were 14 jurors on this case, a civil matter involving a traffic accident. We would all sit through the trial. At its end, two of us would be designated as alternates. These two would not have to deliberate—just be available in case one of the original jurors couldn't continue.

"Please, God, let me be an alternate. But Your will be done...I think..."

The trial ended. The alternates were chosen. I wasn't one of them.

As I headed in dread to the jury room, I offered up one last, desperate prayer. "Please, God, You have to protect me from a lifetime of guilt. Won't You let us reach a verdict I don't have to second-guess?"

God answered that prayer. We reached a decision in just half a day. As I leaped for joy on the porch of faith, my conscience didn't ache at all—just the knee I'd tweaked on a sightseeing jaunt with fellow jurors during one of our lunch breaks. On balance, the week-long experience had been surprisingly pleasant. Best of all, jury duty had lost its terror...or at least most of it.

I served yet another stint on jury duty just months ago. This time it was criminal court, which didn't thrill me. Faltering just slightly with one paw, I kept my three others on the porch of faith as I prayed for God's will over mine.

"I just don't want to be on a murder trial, God."

That's the panel I was picked for.

I had to laugh…even as I saw how God had grown my trust in Him. Mercifully we were told at the start that this wouldn't be a death penalty case. I had my moments, but overall I wasn't nearly as scared as before as I begged for release and yet for His will.

I wasn't chosen for this jury. God let me be excused.

Unlike God, I don't deserve perfect trust from the people and pets in my life. I'm imperfect. I don't always do what's right for them. Sometimes I don't know. Other times I choose my interests over theirs. Perhaps that's one reason I struggle to trust God…because it's hard to conceive of a Being who is free of my own failings.

No matter. God, in His perfect wisdom, knows just how to stretch and grow my faith. He is patient and persistent. He knows taming me will be a lifelong process. He understands that I won't see all things clearly in this world. But one day, when I pass into His presence and see Him as He really is, I will leap from the porch of faith to His arms, doubt free and fully tamed forever.

The LORD is my strength and my shield; my heart trusts in him, and I am helped. My heart leaps for joy and I will give thanks to him in song (Psalm 28:7).

CONSIDER THIS

Is there an area of your life where you're skittish with God instead of trusting? Why do you think this is so? How might you move closer to the porch of faith?

Free to Fly

Obedience Brings Blessings

Do the thing you fear most and
the death of fear is certain.

Mark Twain

Our oldest son was 15 when he begged us to let him stay home that summer. Normally our family spent three weeks at a cabin in Lake Tahoe. The previous year, Sam had spent most of his time complaining or writing postcards to friends saying he was being held captive and to send help. He'd come to hate this annual pilgrimage because his idea of vacation was now quite different from ours. We enjoyed doing quiet and relaxing things at the cabin. Sam craved adventure. Because we didn't want him or us to be miserable, we arranged for an older friend of his to keep him company at our home. They were surfing buddies, so Sam wouldn't have to miss even one wave.

Sam was thrilled to be spared our vacation, even though it meant he was also in charge of our three cats—a little calico named Racky and her much larger son and daughter, Pumpkin and Tiger.

Tiger was a gray tabby who spent a lot of her life being fearful.

She was literally a scaredy-cat. If someone knocked at our front door, she leaped in the air and then made a mad dash upstairs to hide. Even if she was upstairs in our "safe" bedroom, we'd find her later, under the bed. She quaked in terror when the meter reader arrived in our backyard. When Tiger saw him, she stopped in her tracks, eyes wide. Then she scurried deep into some bushes. Fear ruled Tiger's life.

Nevertheless, she was my husband's all-time favorite cat because of her sweetness. She loved to cuddle with us at night. This was the only time Tiger felt safe. As Phil climbed into bed, she would jump on the mattress, walk up beside him, and fling herself prone next to him so that her head was near his face and her body against his belly. That's where she was all night long, between us. Every time either of us would touch her, she'd purr. It was lovely, after awakening in the middle of the night, to fall back to sleep hearing that soft purring sound.

When we left for vacation, we weren't concerned for the other two cats, but we were worried about Tiger. As it turned out, we had good reason to be. After a few days, Sam called to say, "Tiger won't come in. She's living in the bushes." Apparently the combination of us being gone and Sam's friend living in her house was more than she could bear. She felt safer hiding in the bushes than facing her fear. Sam tried to catch her for several days, to no avail, so he decided the only thing he could do was to put her food and water out on the deck each evening. And that's the way it was for those very long three weeks of Tiger's life. Her fear enslaved her.

I had a fear that ruled me for a long time too—a fear of flying. I had developed it early in my marriage. It began on a weekend trip to San Francisco when I felt as if the plane was spinning downward. I grabbed Phil's arm in a panic, but then I noticed no one else was showing any concern. Later on I would learn it was my inner ear misbehaving, but by then the fear was quite entrenched. Because Phil's family lived on the East Coast and we were on the West Coast, I had to fly frequently. I became obsessed with fear about flying for months ahead of time. Then, on the day of the flight, I would board our plane as if I were a captive walking the plank of a pirate ship. Once the horror of takeoff was over, I'd jump with fright at every little noise or change in direction. After each safe landing, if I could have done so, I would have kissed the ground.

Then I teamed with a dear friend to coteach a Bible study class which was part of a national ministry. We alternated being the teaching director and associate for six years. The ministry held a yearly conference to revive and inspire the volunteer teachers in their positions. Only the teaching directors, not the associates, could attend. In the beginning, this event was held alternately on the East and West Coasts. That suited me just fine. It meant I could go on the West Coast years, leaving the East Coast flights to my buddy, who loved flying. Then all that changed. The ministry announced the conference would be held in Florida from then on. They had found an ideal location and had signed a ten-year contract.

When I heard the news, I felt as though I were a balloon that had lost all its air. I was doomed! I knew God had called me to teach, but I hadn't thought flying would be a part of it. I was in a real dilemma; if I stopped teaching, I would be disobedient to God's call on my life, and if I refused the conference, I would be missing out on a very special event. What was I to do?

This was the state in which I found myself when my daughter and I went on our annual trek to the mountains just east of L.A. for a yearly mother/daughter conference. We looked forward to this weekend all year long. I'd loved every one of these events, but at this particular conference God had a great surprise waiting for me.

He was fitting puzzle pieces together to help me decide to battle my fears so I wouldn't be stuck in the bushes of life. The first piece was meeting a special lady that weekend. As we shared our lives, we discovered we were both Bible study teaching directors for the same organization. We were slated to attend the same conference in Florida. She encouraged me to come, promising to pray me through my fears, and we decided to be roommates.

The second puzzle piece was God speaking to my heart. He told me very clearly, "It's time to face your fear!" He brought to my mind Tiger in the bushes, how miserable those three weeks had been, and how happy she could have been inside her house if only she had been courageous enough to go.

It was then that I realized how much I needed to take courage and push myself to be obedient. I told God I would go, and He then provided the last puzzle piece. There was another teaching director who needed to be in Los Angeles a few days before the Florida trip, and she would be on my flight. We arranged to sit together.

The flight to Florida was far easier than I had expected. It was smooth as glass—no turbulence whatsoever. Not only that, but the plane didn't sound strange to me, even once. When I arrived at the conference, the fun I had rooming with my new friend was almost magical. The Florida location was amazing and has since become one of my favorite places on earth. On one side of the conference grounds is a beautiful beach where conch shells wash up with great regularity. On the other, wonderful paths wind through lush trees laden with hanging moss. The conference itself was fabulous.

God richly rewarded me for facing my fear. Something in me knew this was the time. I knew if I had succumbed, not only would I have disappointed my Lord, but fear would have gained more power over me. I'm still not one who says, "Oh, goody!" when I have to fly, but it isn't the battle it once was. I don't obsess anymore before the trip, and I actually enjoy most of it now.

Tiger never did come into our house the whole three weeks we were gone. She let fear rob her of the life she could have had there. Giving in to fear would have robbed me of the life God had for me. I'm so grateful I obeyed His challenge so He could set me free to fly and bless me in His service!

It is for freedom that Christ has set us free. Stand firm, then, and do not let yourselves be burdened again by a yoke of slavery (Galatians 5:1).

CONSIDER THIS

Do you have fears that keep you from experiencing all God has for you? What are they? How have they hindered you? How might God be challenging you to face your fears in obedience to Him?

Jumping from the Helmet

Caring Builds Trust

You cannot do a kindness too soon, for you never know how soon it will be too late.

Ralph Waldo Emerson

We had a whole succession of farm cats when our children were young. Our kids were into rhyming words, so they gave them rhyming names. Sid's kittens were Lester, Chester, and Webster. They were fluffy with gray-and-white stripes, and they lived in a motorcycle helmet. Usually our mother cats found a soft place in the straw beneath a piece of farm equipment to keep their kittens while they were small, but Sid had discovered the blue-and-gold helmet on the garage floor. It was large, with thick black padding inside. She decided to keep her babies there.

One day Steve went outside and found out that Sid had met with an accident. Now her kittens were orphans, too young to care for themselves. Their grandma cat tried to help, but she had no milk to feed them. So our three children came to the rescue. We bought the kitties special bottles and milk. Christy, John, and Karen each got a bottle ready. Then they slowly and quietly crept into the garage, calling the kittens by name. In just seconds, they heard little meows coming from the helmet. They coaxed the kitties out and each child fed one.

The first few times, the kittens were reluctant to leave the safety of their helmet. But they soon realized the children had become their providers. Before long they were jumping from the helmet to greet their human friends. They seemed to know they were not alone because their humans treated them with love and filled their needs. It was quite a picture to see the little ones as they leaped from the helmet one by one and walked in a straight line toward the children. They were grateful. The bonding was strong.

There are many people who, like those kittens, hesitate to jump from their "helmet." They're not sure others love them and want to meet their needs. But like those kitties, they will often respond if someone takes the time to care about them.

A few years ago, our family helped to start a new church. We worshipped with and reached out to many different kinds of people. Steve made a point of meeting newcomers on their first Sunday. When they came back again, he would greet them by name. This became a huge blessing to one gentleman in particular. He had come to our church with great reservations, hiding in his emotional helmet. He'd been hurt before in a church and feared it might happen again. He needed a friend he could depend on. Steve became that person. He took the man and his wife to lunch. He greeted them by name week after week. It doesn't seem like a huge thing, but this man said it changed his life. Steve's new friend felt cared for and loved. He was grateful. The bonding was strong. Like Sid's kittens, he was learning to jump from his helmet.

Jesus met needs and befriended many when He walked this earth. He fed the hungry, healed the sick, and coaxed many from their helmets. One was a Samaritan woman He met at her local well (see John 4). She was shocked when He asked for a drink because Jews looked down on Samaritans and usually wanted nothing to do with them. But Jesus reached out. He offered her living water. He showed her He knew of her sin and shame, and yet He took time to care about her and even revealed Himself to her. She jumped from her helmet and ran to tell others she might have found the Messiah.

If we take a few moments to care for others in Jesus' name, who knows what helmet they might jump from to a more abundant life.

Dear friends, since God so loved us, we also ought to love one another. No one has ever seen God; but if we love one another, God lives in us and his love is made complete in us (1 John 4:11-12).

CONSIDER THIS

Have you ever hidden in a helmet? What about it felt safe? What about it stunted your growth? Who and what coaxed you out? How might you coax others to jump from their helmets by caring about them?

Mooch Mountain

Nothing Is Impossible with God

The life of Jesus is bracketed by two impossibilities: a virgin's womb and an empty tomb.

Peter Larson

There they were! As we opened the door, our friends from church burst through, loaded down with bags of cat food, cat toys, spare bowls, and one very anxious kitty named Mooch who had scratched halfway through his carrier. Mooch was a male four-year-old gray tabby with white markings on his face, neck, and paws. His eyes were wide and frantic that morning.

Mooch had belonged to a dear older friend who had recently gone to heaven. Because we'd loved Connie so much, we were thrilled to adopt the cat she'd adored. And we'd been thinking about introducing a new cat or kitten to our ten-year-old jet-black female kitty, Midnight. Her lifelong pal, our beloved Pumpkin, had passed away a few months earlier, and she was now an only cat.

We hoped that being different sexes would help our two kitties get along. We were wrong! In the next days and weeks, we tried everything we knew to break the ice—to no avail. We rubbed each cat down with a towel and traded towels to introduce the new scent. We closed Mooch in a room and let him and Midnight sniff each other through the crack beneath the door. We let them eye each other with a screen door or glass door between them. Whenever we allowed them in an area together, we put down a bowl of tuna for each. We even sprayed our home with a "cat neutral" scent. I don't know what else we could have done to ease their adjustment.

After about a month of such efforts, one day the unthinkable happened. Phil carried Mooch to the side door to let him out while I took my post at the back door to let Midnight in. This time, however, as soon as Mooch's paws hit the ground, he turned tail and raced back past Phil to confront Midnight in the living room. She let out a screech I hope to never hear again and lunged at him, bristling. Mooch turned and fled up the stairs, but he didn't quite make it to the safety of what was by now his room. Midnight beat him to it, and by the time I reached the stair landing they had become one growling ball of fur rolling toward me down the steps in a hostile embrace. They hit the floor near me, claws and paws everywhere, looking just like a cat fight in a cartoon, and kept rolling to the bottom of the stairs where, thankfully, they fled in different directions. Midnight dove under a bed in the back downstairs bedroom. Mooch raced for the door to escape.

I sat on the steps and bawled my eyes out. What had we done? Had we made an awful mistake in taking this cat?

We've had three more catfights similar to the first one. It seems impossible that Mooch and Midnight will ever coexist, let alone become friends. But as I've gone over and over the details of how we got Mooch, I've come to the same conclusion again and again: God was in it. Phil and I were praying for just the right cat. We agreed that Mooch was the one. We wanted to take him because we had loved Connie. And Midnight had been used to having other feline companions. She had shared our home with our three older cats most of her life, till one by one they had all passed away.

Everything seemed to fit together, like puzzle pieces. But this wasn't working!

And then, I remembered the verse, "Nothing is impossible with God" (Luke 1:37).

Jesus made this point to His disciples in Matthew 17. He'd just cast a demon out of a boy after they had tried and failed. They asked Him why they'd had no success. Jesus replied, "Because you have so little faith. I tell you the truth, if you have faith as small as a mustard seed, you can say to this mountain, 'Move from here to there' and it will move. Nothing will be impossible for you" (Matthew 17:20).

Mooch and Midnight becoming friends looked like an immovable mountain. But it wasn't the first such mountain Phil and I had faced. Twenty-five years earlier, we had tried to adopt a little girl, and that too had seemed impossible.

Abortion had been recently legalized, so the number of available infants had dropped drastically. We'd already adopted a baby boy through our local county agency; then I got pregnant and had a second son. Our boys were only ten months apart. With two babies, we were too busy to even think of adopting a daughter for a time. When we did inquire, the agency told us we weren't eligible for an infant. Infants were defined as birth through age two. Due to the scarcity of babies, an age limit had been set for prospective parents. Phil was 43 and I was 35. We had grown too old. Our ages stood like a mountain between us and our hearts' desire.

I had become a Christian after my boys were born, and was in a Bible study group. My friends there knew God better than I did. When I shared this, they said they would pray. They told me to walk by faith; that God could do the impossible—even move a mountain if it was in His will. I took their advice, and I released my dream of a daughter to Him. I recall one prayer in particular. I told the Lord, "If You want me to have a daughter I would love that, but if it's not Your will for me, I'm content with my two boys."

A couple of years passed. One day a little redheaded girl was dedicated at our church. My heart leaped as I saw her. I thought, "I'd sure love to have a redheaded daughter." It was just a fleeting thought. It didn't cross my mind again until the county agency called to tell us they were considering us for a little girl. Then they said, "She's 16 months old and she's a carrottop!"

At that moment I knew God had moved the mountain. We learned later that they had matched Sarah up with several other couples; she even went home with one of them for a day. But she hadn't bonded as they had hoped—so the agency tried us.

The new mountain was our bonding with Sarah. I took that one to my Bible study group too. Once again, they reminded me that "nothing is impossible with God." By now I was looking for God's miracles, so I went to the foster mom's house expecting God to move this new mountain. I knew this redhead was mine!

Sarah's social worker had warned me about coming on too strong with her. She cautioned that Sarah liked men, but not women, so I shouldn't be too aggressive when I met her. Phil was holding a toy we had brought for her, and she climbed right into his lap to play with it. I sat on my hands. After some getting acquainted time, we were encouraged to take Sarah out for a walk. On the way home she grew tired, and I asked if I could hold her. She consented, so I picked her up. The social worker had a mile-wide grin when she saw us return with Sarah content in my arms.

I took a month to be home with Sarah and not be separated at all. It was a glorious time as the Lord tightly bonded us to each other. He had moved mountains to bring us together in the first place, so I knew He would be in the adjustment period.

Sarah has grown up into a wonderful young woman. We continue to be close. She's now married and expecting her first child. We can hardly wait to meet our new grandson.

I can also hardly wait to see how God will move our "Mooch mountain." I've seen Him work before and expect Him to again. I'm walking by faith and not by sight as I gaze not at the mountain's size, but my far bigger God for whom nothing is impossible.

I tell you the truth, anyone who has faith in me will do what I have been doing. He will do even greater things than these, because I am going to the Father (John 14:12).

CONSIDER THIS

Has God ever called you to walk by faith and believe Him for something even though all the evidence screamed otherwise? What happened? How did it affect your relationship with Him? Where do you need to walk by faith, not sight, in your life right now?

The Licked-up Glory

Seek God's Glory, Not Yours

It is amazing what you can accomplish
if you do not care who gets the credit.

Harry S. Truman

When Kitty lived mainly in the house, she found ways to entertain herself that made her happy and content. One day she played with a fly on the living room window. Although it didn't appear to be any fun at all for the fly, Kitty batted at it first with one paw and then the other. She tried to bite it. She even licked it a little. Finally she pinned it to the window with her paw—only to release it again. This went on for what seemed like hours.

Kitty seemed rather proud of her work, but I doubt the poor fly could have flown away in the end. It never got the chance. While Kitty continued to swipe at it, Max, our Boston Terrier, sat patiently watching. All at once he dashed to the window and licked up the fly with one swipe of his tongue. Then he strolled away while Kitty just sat there, astounded. In a flash, all she'd worked for was licked up by someone else.

Kitty's experience made me ponder how we humans often

work hard on something, only to have others swoop in and lick up the glory. Our family worked together on countless projects. We often pitched in with school band events in the city where we live. Steve would haul a huge grill to a school for a cookout. I'd do the shopping. Steve and several others would make the meal. They'd barbecue meat for hundreds of people. Our three kids would help set up the tables. They'd lug a large roll of craft paper around, cutting and taping until every table was covered. Then they'd set out utensils and napkins for all the guests.

We felt that working together like this to help others was good for our kids, even though it took many hours. It was a great way to teach them to be servants. Serving others is something God commands. We were often some of the first to arrive and the last to leave. Many other families pitched in for long hours as well, but there were always the people who showed up late and helped for just a short time, yet somehow managed to lick up all the thanks.

Even though this wasn't exactly fair, Steve and I decided glory wasn't part of the plan. The work needed doing. It was good for our kids to be involved. We all had a fun time and went home tired, taught, and content.

I've had to learn to let go of the glory on my personal projects too. I have worked on several films in the past few years. I've helped with anything that needed doing—casting, producing, designing sets, finding locations, assisting the actors.

I recall one particular film where I helped the producers behind the scenes. They asked me to find them locations, and I did. Once they needed extras for a scene, and I found more than 70 people. They were so appreciative, and that felt wonderful. But the film's director didn't know what I'd done. When the formal, public thank-you's were said at the end of the shoot, others licked up the glory for my hard work.

I thought about that for a while, and I decided I didn't really do all that work for that director. This film was for the Lord. I did it for Him. Paul urges us all to take this approach when he writes,

"Whatever you do, work at it with all your heart, as working for the Lord, not for men, since you know that you will receive an inheritance from the Lord as a reward. It is the Lord Christ you are serving" (Colossians 3:23-24).

I couldn't ask her, but I always felt Kitty walked away from that fly feeling cheated. I didn't feel cheated. I went home with a smile. Even if I didn't get full credit, Jesus got the glory in the end, and that's what mattered most.

So whether you eat or drink or whatever you do, do it all for the glory of God (1 Corinthians 10:31).

CONSIDER THIS

Have you ever worked hard on something, only to have the credit for it licked up by someone else? How did you feel? What did you do? Have you ever licked up someone else's glory? Whose glory are you most concerned with in your current work or ministry, your own or the Lord's?

Steps of Faith

God Helps Us Through Tough Times

A mighty fortress is our God, a bulwark never failing; Our helper He, amid the flood of mortal ills prevailing.

Martin Luther

Pumpkin was fading. Our beautiful orange tabby had been with us for nearly 20 years. We'd witnessed the miracle of his birth right in our upstairs bedroom. Now Phil and I were watching his demise.

Of all our cats, Pumpkin had been our closest companion. He just liked being near us wherever we were. He'd come and find us in the house or yard and then curl up close by and go to sleep. If we were gone when he awoke, he'd rouse himself and come looking for us again.

At this point in his life, however, he didn't follow us anymore. Once he'd taken care of his daily necessities, he jumped up on a cushioned dining room chair. He was content to remain there all day. He'd come down to eat a few bites of his dinner and then return to his chair again. That was his pattern for nearly three months.

Pumpkin's vet said he was in no pain, and he might just go to sleep one day and not wake up. We hoped for that for him, much as we hated to lose him. We didn't want him to suffer. Each day we'd sit with him and pet him to let him know we still loved him. Each night before we went upstairs, we'd stroke his head and say goodbye, just in case it might be the last time.

I'm the early bird in our home. When I woke in the morning during those months, I wondered if Pumpkin would still be alive. I walked to the stairs with great trepidation, praying for the courage to descend because I had no idea what I might find below.

There was another time in my life, a time before Pumpkin was born, when I asked for courage to descend those same stairs. Someone was dying then too—my precious mother.

Mom had been a big part of our family even before we moved her into our home. She lived only a few miles away. We had three active children, ages twelve, eleven, and five. She was very involved with them. But as time passed, we saw Mom fading. She was losing certain skills for independent living. My husband suggested that Mom should move in with us, and my brothers agreed.

We added an upstairs onto our home and began life as a new family of six. Mom and our daughter had bedrooms on the first floor. Our five-year-old was elated to have her grandma just down the hall from her. We all felt quite comfortable together. We hoped to enjoy Mom for at least ten years. But that was not to be. She lived with us for only one.

At first it was wonderful. Mom played the piano while I cooked dinner. She read to our daughter at bedtime. She was a delight for me as well. Our relationship was very special. Sometimes we talked about her "kids." Mom had taught school for 30 years and she loved her students as if they were her own children. She loved sharing about the high school kids who came back to visit her to tell her they still remembered her kindness as their first grade teacher. Sometimes we talked about her grandchildren. She had eight, including our three. Each was as special to her as if she had only one. And we talked about Jesus, whom she had met late in her life.

She still couldn't get over the reality of having a relationship with Him, and she sang to Him or played hymns as often as she could.

Sadly, Mom was sicker than any of us knew when she came to live with us. The cancer she had so valiantly fought a decade before had returned. Soon she would also be diagnosed with Alzheimer's disease. It was one of the darkest periods of my life. But God was there. I had asked Jesus into my life six years before. I knew He was real. Now I was to learn He is "an ever-present help in trouble" (Psalm 46:1).

During the last three months of Mom's life, I prayed for courage each day as I stood at the top of the stairs. The hospice nurses had said she could die at any time. As with Pumpkin, I didn't know what I'd find when I descended those steps each morning. For nearly three months, Mom lay in her bed, too removed from us by Alzheimer's disease for any conversation. But I sat and talked with her anyway. I visited with her as if she were able to take it all in. I petted her hair, fought back the tears, and said "good night" (meaning "goodbye") each evening.

Then, after I got everyone settled, I went out on my veranda and wept buckets as I poured out my complaints to the Lord. I even changed from calling Him Lord or Father to calling Him Master because I felt so much like a slave to my circumstances.

He took all my complaints, all my anger and all my confusion, and He never left me. Not only that, but He showed me in miraculous ways that He was with me in this sorrow. The last month of Mom's life, I awoke every morning to music—music I can't really describe. It was amazing and wondrous music, complete with instruments and voices I'm certain were heavenly. I truly believe that God, in His goodness to me in this extremely difficult time, pulled back the curtain that separates earth from heaven so I could experience those heavenly sounds in the moments when I regained consciousness after a night's sleep. They would fade away gradually as I opened my eyes to the new day.

Perhaps as miraculous was the courage I felt as I descended the stairs to see if Mom was still alive. It also felt as though it was from heaven. My sweet mother died peacefully one night in her sleep. On that night, at around 4:00 a.m., my husband woke up with me and said, "Let's check on Mom." That in itself was unusual because he was a sound sleeper and almost always slept through till morning. We descended the stairs together and peeked into her room. It was obvious that she was no longer in that sad body. She had gone to be with her Savior. I believe God awakened my husband, knowing Phil's presence would minister to me so I wouldn't feel alone. I saw this as God taking care of me through my husband. He called the hospice people and I called my family, and together we thanked God for taking her.

Life got back to normal. The music I had heard upon awakening ceased. The prayers for courage at the top of the stairs ceased as well. But my faith increased. It took off like a rocket at blastoff. I learned that God gives His children exactly what we need, when we need it. I didn't need the celestial chorus anymore. I didn't need courage to face the steps. Not then…

Not till Pumpkin was dying.

When I faced this new loss, I knew I'd receive the courage I prayed for at the top of the stairs. God had given it to me for Mom's death. He would do so again.

As it happened, Pumpkin didn't die on the dining room chair. He died peacefully in our vet's office. He suffered for just one night, after which we felt it kindest to have him put down. That night my dear husband slept on the floor close to Pumpkin so he would know we were still with him.

It takes courage to face the loss of a loved one, whether it's a pet or a person. But we don't have to face death or life or any tough time alone. God will be "an ever-present help in trouble," supplying the strength and comfort we need, if we will only call on Him.

You, O God, do see trouble and grief; you consider it to take it in hand. The victim commits himself to you; you are the helper of the fatherless (Psalm 10:14).

CONSIDER THIS

Has God ever been your "help in trouble?" How did He meet your needs? What happened to your faith as a result?

God works through His people. How might He use you to minister to someone in crisis?

In This World We Will Have Hairballs

God Is Greater than Our Troubles

Sometimes the littlest things in life are the hardest to take. You can sit on a mountain more comfortably than on a tack.

Author Unknown

My cat Misty licks my hair. She comes up behind me when I'm sprawled on the couch and goes at it with her rough little tongue. It's not that she mistakes my hair for some kind of kitty lollipop. She's probably trying to groom me as she would her feline friends. She's treating me as one of her own. That's the way cats bathe themselves and each other. But in so doing, they may lick up some fur and swallow it. That's how they get hairballs.

Hairballs are no fun for a feline, as anyone knows who has ever heard cats vocalize while expelling them. They gag and cough. At times they make prehistoric noises. Thankfully, things are usually not as bad as they sound. While some hairballs can cause serious problems, most are minor and cause only momentary discomfort. If I could walk this earth as a kitty and speak Misty's language, I'd tell her that. I'd say, "It's a hazard of being a cat. In this world, you will have hairballs."

When God the Son walked this earth as a man and spoke human language, He said we'd have hairballs too.

In John 16 Jesus is preparing His disciples for His imminent crucifixion. The chapter concludes with these words from our Lord: "In this world you will have trouble. But take heart! I have overcome the world" (John 16:33).

One of the hazards of being a human in our fallen world is that we will have trials, both big and small. Oddly enough, it's in dealing with life's minor irritations that I sometimes fail most dismally to rely on God.

I recall one recent bad hairball day. It started with stepping on the bathroom scale. My weight was up. Though it wasn't by much, this hairball got me down.

My agitation heightened when I received some disconcerting news about an impending poor decision by a family member. This was a much bigger hairball. Still, God could handle it too, couldn't He? But instead of resting in my Lord, I coughed and gagged and made prehistoric sounds on the phone to my relative.

Even as I seethed, a brand-new hairball was headed my way. My plumber had two of his men in my backyard, digging. Pooling water had suggested a slow leak in a mainline pipe. He'd capped off the water flow to the area and recommended bypassing the problem. Now his guys were searching for the buried pipe. But hours later the men had struck out...and racked up quite a labor bill in the process.

Somehow I kept my cool with them—arranging with my gardeners to dig further at a lower hourly rate. But this frustration primed me to boil over at the day's final hairball. My dishwasher had refused to turn on. I had it on a protection plan. I'd had to wait for service. Now I learned I must wait days more for a part. I did more spitting and sputtering and made more prehistoric sounds as I announced that the time frame was unacceptable—realizing all the while that I ought to just do the piled dishes and not be a spoiled brat.

I was reacting out of all proportion to the hairballs I was having. If Misty or my other cats do this, it's quite understandable. My cats don't know that "this, too, shall pass." They don't realize their discomfort is just temporary. They don't know I have hairball medicine I can give them if need be. So if they sometimes sound like the world is ending when they have a hairball, who am I to blame them?

But I know that pipes and dishwashers get fixed. And I know that even far greater problems are but momentary afflictions in the eternal scheme of things. I know what Jesus did after talking with His disciples on that long-ago day. He went to the cross and died for my sins. He overcame sin and death for me. His blood is the ultimate hairball medicine. And though I'll have troubles in this life, when I pass into God's presence I'll be done with them forever.

The hairballs I struggled with that day have mostly passed. My relative didn't make that bad decision after all. I did the dirty dishes, and days later, the dishwasher was fixed. So was the backyard pipe, and the plumber adjusted the bill in my favor. My weight will be an ongoing issue, and I'll have new hairballs to deal with too. But I'll keep these blips on my radar in better perspective if I focus on God.

Jesus told His disciples that despite life's troubles, they could still have peace—in Him. He said He was greater than anything they could face. That's true for me too. So I will hold fast to the One who has overcome the world—and try not to let life's hairballs get me down.

Peace I leave with you; my peace I give you. I do not give to you as the world gives. Do not let your hearts be troubled and do not be afraid (John 14:27).

CONSIDER THIS

Which of life's hairballs cause you most discomfort? How do you deal with them now? What are the results? How might focusing on God make things better?

Christmas Treed

Hold Fast Its True Meaning

Christmas began in the heart of God. It is complete only when it reaches the heart of man.

AUTHOR UNKNOWN

Christmas was always a special time in our family when I was growing up. On Christmas Eve we had a wonderful program at our church. The story of the first Christmas was told by children. This particular year I played the angel who told the shepherds to go find the babe wrapped in swaddling clothes, lying in a manger. Afterward, everyone was given a bag of nuts and candy. There was lots of hugging and hearty handshaking. This was the beginning of Christmas.

I went to bed feeling too excited to sleep, but I must have dozed off. Next thing I knew, it was Christmas morning. I jumped out of bed and went to the kitchen. Dad was drinking coffee. Mom was cooking up a special Christmas breakfast. After hugging them, I ran to the living room to see our Christmas tree. Lots of old glass ornaments hung on it proudly, along with some newer ones. They were joined by handmade ornaments made throughout the years by every child in our family—some out of dough, some out of paper, all cherished.

As I was enjoying our tree, I noticed our cat Macee sitting on the front lawn, looking in at me. Macee wasn't allowed in the house as a rule. But once in a while, if I pleaded politely and promised to hold her, Mom would permit it. Christmas morning was one of those times. With Mom's consent, I let her in and scooped her into my arms.

By then everybody else was awake and we gathered in the living room. I held Macee on my lap, as Mom required. Dad always read the Christmas story from the Bible before we opened presents. As I listened, I forgot the cat. At some point, she must have slipped off my lap. When I noticed her again, she was headed for the tree. I didn't want to interrupt Dad, so I just watched her. She stepped softly over the presents without bothering them. She had noticed the ornaments and started up the tree to get one.

I held my breath as Macee climbed higher and higher. When she'd nearly reached the top, the tree tipped over. It crashed onto the presents, shedding its beautiful ornaments all over the room. Mom let out her classic shriek of surprise: "OOOOHHH OOOOHHH!" Dad closed the Bible and barked, "Get that cat out of this house…NOW!"

Everyone scrambled to catch poor Macee. Then, out of nowhere, Dad started laughing. First he chuckled. Then he guffawed. Mom began laughing too. The rest of us joined in. We let Macee out and cleaned up the mess. Then we opened our presents. I don't remember what I got for Christmas or what I gave. But I'll never forget how we didn't let a fallen tree wreck its true meaning. Dad even allowed Macee back inside a bit later.

Many years afterward, my husband and I were enjoying Christmas in our own home with our daughter Christy. She was only two years old and very curious about everything. As we were wrapping presents in the den, Christy toddled to the living room to look at the Christmas tree. We don't know what she did exactly, but suddenly the tree went tumbling down. Christy squealed and ran into the den. She looked up at us with eyes big as saucers and yelled in terror, "WHAT DID YOU DO?"

Her astonishment was so cute that we just went with it. One of us said, "What did YOU do, Christy?" She took us into the living room and showed us the fallen tree. Then she started crying. We just hugged her and smiled. Then Steve took her in his arms. "Christy, did you get hurt?" he asked. "No," she sniffled. "Accidents happen, honey. Let's just clean it up," he told her. Christy smiled and we all worked until the tree was back up and looking pretty. Once again a fallen Christmas tree was not going to ruin the true meaning of Christmas. Our focus was on Jesus and His birth, not a few broken ornaments.

There are other things that threaten to "pull the Christmas tree down" in our lives—to switch our focus off the real meaning of Christmas. Being overly concerned with presents and parties can do this. So can family problems and crisis events. One such crisis in our lives became one of our most memorable Christmases.

I am the youngest of five children. I have three sisters and one brother. Eleven years ago, my brother, Darrell, developed a heart problem. He was advised to go to a hospital near San Francisco for surgery, a three-hour drive from his home. It was originally scheduled for the day after Christmas. But, after careful consideration, his doctors decided they'd better move the operation up to Christmas Day.

Darrell made the trip by ambulance. Those of us who could drove up to be with him. We prayed with him before the surgery. It was hard to let him go, but we had to. We and our families all stayed near or in a special waiting room. The grown-ups prayed and visited. The kids played and also joined in prayer. After several hours, the doctor came out and told us Darrell had survived. It had been a difficult operation, but the doctor felt something had carried him through. We told him it was prayer.

That year we ate Christmas dinner in the hospital cafeteria. It wasn't exactly what we had planned, but we were so thankful and joyful over Darrell that we actually enjoyed it. Afterward, we decided to have Christmas in our hotel. We asked the cashier for some white paper doilies of the type they used under coffee cups. At a local store we bought flat, round, colored candies and some foil-wrapped chocolates. Using gum, we stuck the doilies on a glass hotel room door in the shape of a Christmas tree. We tinkered with the candies, wrapping them to form little nativity scenes—using toothpicks to help the tiny images stay strong. Then we all gathered, gave thanks for Darrell, and sang Christmas carols. Afterward, the kids dressed up in sheets and pillowcases to put on a Christmas play. We had someone for every part, and the baby of the family got to be Jesus. Being together in one small hotel room celebrating Christmas so uniquely made for a Christmas memory we will always cherish.

Macee and Christy each toppled a tree. Darrell toppled Christmas in a grander way, but it didn't knock the season's true meaning from our hearts; in fact, it made it even more true. The reason for Christmas isn't trees, meals, and presents—much as we enjoy them. It's to celebrate the One who was born in a manger and died on a cross to topple death so we could be raised to spend eternity with Him.

The angel said to them, "Do not be afraid. I bring you good news of great joy that will be for all the people. Today in the town of David a Savior has been born to you; he is Christ the Lord" (Luke 2:10-11).

CONSIDER THIS

What events or attitudes tend to knock the true meaning of Christmas from your heart? How might you regain your focus on the Lord? What was your most memorable Christmas, and why?

Part III

To Hiss or Not to Hiss?

God Cleanses and Refines Us

RAJAH

Picture Purr-fect

Look at Life from God's Perspective

If you do not raise your eyes you will
think you are the highest point.

Antonio Porchia

Rajah was a picture purr-fect kitten. She was beautiful and appeared to pose every time she saw a camera. We have photos of her sitting on the dining room table beside a vase of flowers. We have a shot of her on the piano. And of course there are many pictures of Rajah being held by those who loved her. But my favorite is of Rajah actually perched up on a fishbowl. She would sit there for hours watching the fish swim around. From her seat up above, she could see everything that was going on in the water.

Although this made for a great picture, I'm sure the fish were not at all happy about Rajah's antics. Here they were, swimming in their nice safe comfortable bowl, and along comes a huge cat, staring down at them. Of course, their view was limited, and so was their comprehension. But if they could have understood their plight, they probably would have felt trapped.

I also have to wonder what might have happened if those fish had a chance to be lifted out of their bowl and sit on top, looking down. If they'd had Rajah's view of their world, I can only imagine how their perspective might have changed!

There are times in my life when I feel as though I live in a fishbowl, swimming around in circles, trapped by my circumstances. I had such moments the first time I worked on a feature film.

Helping to produce the film was an incredible experience. I knew very little about making a film at the start. So much was new to me, but I felt led by God to do this, and the writer-director of the film felt I should work for him too.

Even though I knew God sent me there, it didn't take me long to allow everyone and everything else to take over my thoughts. There were sets to be designed, props to find, characters to cast, people to be fed, locations to be found. And I had many miles to travel. Sometimes after a long day of filming I had to drive three hours to get home. It was at those moments that I jumped into the fishbowl. I'd spend those three hours going over all the negative things that had happened that day. I would tell myself that it was time to quit. I felt overwhelmed by murky water and other fish crowding in on me, and I couldn't see much else.

But God, in His infinite mercy and grace, didn't leave me in that fishbowl. Through His Spirit and His Word, He lifted me up to sit atop the bowl with Him. He nudged me to view things from His perspective, which gave me a very different picture. Of course, I couldn't know everything He did, but from that vantage point I once again caught sight of why He had me there. It wasn't to build up my ego or make the director look good. It was to serve my heavenly Father.

Sitting on top of the fishbowl, I viewed everyone in a different way. I saw that those who knew the Lord needed encouraging. Those who didn't know Him needed to see Him through me. When I sat on top of the fishbowl, it was so much easier to give it all to God and allow Him to work through me. Consequently, I made some dear friends from the film and learned a great deal about producing. And I felt that God had used me in a positive way.

Ephesians 2:6 says, "God raised us up with Christ and seated us with him in the heavenly realms in Christ Jesus." From the top of the fishbowl we can have a Romans 12:2 mentality: "Do not conform any longer to the pattern of this world, but be transformed by the renewing of your mind. Then you will be able to test and approve what God's will is—his good, pleasing and perfect will."

Rajah sitting on top of the fishbowl is a great visual to remind me that I'm not just a fish swimming in circles. I'm God's child, and I can watch from the top with Him. Rather than let the world cloud my vision, I can ask God to focus the eyes of my heart—so I can see clearly and live not trapped, but triumphant!

The wisdom of this world is foolishness in God's sight (1 Corinthians 3:19).

CONSIDER THIS

Is there an area of your life where you feel as though you're swimming in a fishbowl? How might God's perspective differ from yours? How might this affect your attitude and actions in your situation?

A Lunge in Time

False Assumptions Can Hurt

Assumptions are the
termites of relationships.

Henry Winkler

I knew Barney was a bit persnickety, but I never dreamed he could morph into an attack cat. So I had no qualms about Cindy being in my house without me. She knew all my puppies and kitties well. What's more, her passion was animal rescue. She'd handled all sorts of animal-related situations.

She was about to encounter a new one.

Cindy is a fabulous designer. She often helps me decorate for Christmas, and that was her purpose in my home this day. I'd planned to be with her, but a close friend had died, and the family needed me. It didn't matter. She knew where everything was. She started opening cabinets and pulling out Christmas things.

That's when Barney started acting weird.

We guessed later that he must have been spooked by the rustling of bags and papers as she rummaged through the decorations. But at the time, she didn't see her danger. She realized he didn't seem too pleased, but she thought since he knew her, things would be okay. Clearly, Barney thought otherwise. He must have assumed she might do him harm. Suddenly, he lunged and bit her arm.

Fortunately, Barney didn't do serious damage, but he did draw blood. Poor Cindy had never posed a threat to him, but he had jumped to a false conclusion and done something hurtful as a result.

I have also jumped to a wrong conclusion about a friend. Though I haven't literally lunged and bitten, I've gone on the attack verbally—as I did with Chelsea.

Chelsea was living in a spare bedroom of my home, at my invitation. I'd thought it would help both of us. She'd had some financial ups and downs and needed to catch her breath. I needed to spend more time with my mom, whose health had had its ups and downs too. Chelsea loved animals and was totally trustworthy. I could go to Mom's at a moment's notice and feel comfortable leaving her in charge. We also both loved the Lord and could pray for each other.

The arrangement worked. Blessings multiplied. So, in time, did Chelsea's stuff.

I'd given Chelsea some storage space in the garage when she moved in. But it's hard to cram your whole life into one room. As her living space filled up, bit by bit she tried to fit more of her things downstairs. It started to bug me. I was feeling territorial, like my cats. Finally, I declared the garage maxed out.

I went off on vacation. When I returned, I thought I noticed more creeping clutter.

I knew I should probably muzzle myself, but the impulse to pounce was strong. Chelsea had gone away for a couple of days. I left a message on her answering machine. Though I managed to temper my words just a bit, my frustration was palpable.

After Chelsea came back home, she didn't respond to my message at first. But a day or so later she stopped me in the hall. By then I was having second thoughts about what I had said. She told me she hadn't even heard it all—most of it had somehow not recorded or had been erased. But enough remained that she knew it had to do with the garage.

I told her how the new clutter had bugged me. And she said it wasn't hers!

It was then I remembered that I'd put a few more of my own things down there right before my trip. I had jumped to a completely false conclusion. Like Barney, I had gone on the attack based on a wrong assumption.

Fortunately, Chelsea forgave me, and the bite did no lasting harm to our friendship. We even wondered if God had deleted some of my verbal teeth marks from her message machine as a protective measure. Chelsea had been well aware of my frustration and was getting back on her financial feet. She told me she'd started apartment hunting. Soon after, she got a place of her own. We each have more room now, and we're still great friends.

I was fortunate with Chelsea. The destructive effects of pouncing on someone can be far worse. We are all tempted to yield to fear, anger, or frustration; make assumptions; and leap into action. But Scripture urges us to err on the side of grace. Paul wrote to the Corinthians that love "is not easily angered, it keeps no record of wrongs...It always protects, always trusts, always hopes, always perseveres" (1 Corinthians 13:5,7).

God in His mercy can heal bites, but it's far better to prevent them. So the next time you're tempted to jump to a negative conclusion, love before you leap.

The LORD is compassionate and gracious, slow to anger, abounding in love (Psalm 103:8).

CONSIDER THIS

What triggers tempt you to jump to conclusions that might prove false and say things that might prove hurtful? How has this affected you and others? What might help you to love before you leap instead?

The Almost Never-Ending Bite

Beware of Spiritual Infection

A little lie can travel half way
round the world while Truth is
still lacing up her boots.

Mark Twain

Pumpkin fancied himself the king of Woodgreen Street. He sat in one particular spot on our front walkway as if on a throne, presiding over the neighborhood. His domain did not go unchallenged, however. Other male cats battled for the title, so we endured many a loud, screeching turf war.

After one particularly fierce fight, the driveway was so littered with fur you would have thought the two cats involved were running around naked. This wasn't the case—and Pumpkin seemed fine at first. But over the next few weeks he became lethargic. He didn't bound downstairs for his breakfast; he plodded. He didn't eat as much as usual, and he was strangely disinterested in the goings-on of our busy household. We took him to our veterinarian to find out what was wrong. After giving Pumpkin a careful exam and questioning us about any recent catfights, the vet said he feared a cat bite had resulted in an infection. He asked permission to do surgery to confirm his suspicions and deal with the problem.

As it turned out, Pumpkin had an infection that was raging throughout his little body. Afterward, the vet told us we had been right to agree to the procedure. He had found pus everywhere. He had cleaned out as much as he could, and what was left could be cured with antibiotics. Though the infection had started small, it had festered and grown to such an extent that without such aggressive treatment, Pumpkin wouldn't have become well.

Spiritual infections can also start small and fester and grow. My friend Stephanie got one of these. It began with a spiritual bite—a random thought about God that grew into a raging infection of wrong doctrine.

Stephanie was excelling in her studies as a college psych major. She was also gaining victory in some personal struggles. She had a therapist she adored who was helping her. But then a change occurred. Because of certain rules at school, she had to give up this stellar therapist. Stephanie was devastated. As she wrestled with her pain, a thought came into her mind: "God is taking her away because He's mean!"

That thought penetrated deeply, just as the bite Pumpkin received in his fight had done. And, just as Pumpkin's bite had spread infection throughout his body, Stephanie's bite spread infection throughout her soul and covered her heart in darkness.

Stephanie didn't have any spiritual antibiotics to help her. She had believed in Jesus as a teen, but the doctrine she received didn't include passages such as, "We demolish arguments and every pretension that sets itself up against the knowledge of God, and we take captive every thought to make it obedient to Christ" (2 Corinthians 10:5). The thought of God being mean festered and grew unchecked because Stephanie didn't understand that the thought came from the enemy of her soul who desired to rob her of her faith.

When I met Stephanie, her countenance was sad. Her belief

that God was mean had grown into a raging infection of hopelessness. My heart ached for her, and I put her in my prayers. I invited her to a Bible study, and to my great delight, she came. That was when God began to do surgery on her infection with His scalpel of truth. That and regular doses of His Word and His love, made real through His people, are doing a healing work in her life.

Millennia ago God made a special garden for the only beings He created in His own image—Adam and Eve. Everything in Eden was beauty and truth, but then the serpent came to confuse them. He tempted and deceived them by giving them a spiritual bite. He told them God was holding out on them. He urged them to eat of the only fruit in the garden forbidden to them. We all know the result of his cunning. Eve took the bait and fell for the lie. She ate…and Adam ate with her. That lie brought an infection of sin which caused separation from God—a separation that continues to this day. The only cure for that separation is faith in the Savior God sent to heal us and bring us back to Him. Jesus said, "I am the way and the truth and the life. No one comes to the Father except through me" (John 14:6).

The serpent—or devil, as we now know him—employs the same tactics today, deceiving and tempting us to believe wrong things about God. None of us is immune from the thoughts that swirl through our minds, but we don't have to let them bite and infect us. As Martin Luther reportedly said, "You can't keep the birds from flying over your head, but you can keep them from building a nest in your hair." That's why we're to take our thoughts captive to Christ, and why Paul urges us to "be transformed by the renewing of your mind" (Romans 12:2).

Neither Pumpkin nor Stephanie could have healed themselves of their infections; they both needed outside help. Thanks to his wonderful vet, Pumpkin recovered completely and went on to live a long, happy life. Thanks to Stephanie's Great Physician, she now has a renewed excitement for the Lord and is looking forward to the future He has planned for her.

I will repay you for the years the locusts have eaten (Joel 2:25).

CONSIDER THIS

Have you ever found yourself believing an error about God? How did it infect your faith? What healed this bite? How might you guard against spiritual infection in the future?

Saved By a Watchcat

Heed Wise Warnings

Better a poor but wise youth than an
old but foolish king who no longer
knows how to take warning.

Ecclesiastes 4:13

Zeke wasn't my cat. He belonged to a friend I'd invited to share my new townhome. I wanted more company than just my own cat, Benji. Two days after Ann and I moved in with our four-foots, Zeke proved he had more in common with his Old Testament namesake, the prophet Ezekiel, than either of us dreamed.

It was late November and I'd been to a special store with my aunt to buy Christmas decorations. When I got home that night, Ann was in her room asleep. I noticed that the toilet was running in the downstairs powder room next to the kitchen, but I was exhausted. I figured I could deal with it in the morning and went up to bed.

No such luck! It was still the wee hours when Ann came into my room to get me. Zeke had pawed and pestered her awake and wouldn't let her be. Finally she'd gone downstairs with him to see what he wanted, and she had found water seeping from that toilet through the bathroom and into the kitchen.

The last thing I wanted at 2:30 a.m. was to crawl out of bed. At first I resisted. This could wait a few more hours, couldn't it?

Ann thought of the brand-new vinyl flooring in the powder room and kitchen, the new carpeting in the adjoining dining room, the still-unpacked boxes from our move whose bottoms were getting soaked, and headed back downstairs to grab a mop. Soon she returned. The flooding was worse.

Heeding Zeke's and Ann's warnings, I went downstairs, fumbled through the yellow pages, and called an emergency plumber. A voice at the other end of the phone helped me find the toilet's shut-off valve. I cranked it. The voice asked if the water had stopped flowing.

It hadn't!

The plumber came, and he couldn't stem the tide of toilet water, either. My night's sleep was over, and I wasn't alone. My townhouse was one of six attached units. The building was new. We called the Realtor, and by 6 a.m. the builder was on site. I'd been to the store to buy flood supplies, and we laid a trail of towels from the kitchen through the dining room and living room to the front door. I still have an image of our poor builder navigating that trail on his knees and elbows to make sure he didn't get dirt on our new carpeting.

The problem was identified at last. A power pole had been moved in putting up our building. When it was replaced, it was put through a sewer line. No one had a clue until several owners moved into their places the same week and began to use the plumbing. Though we'd found trouble first, there was leakage elsewhere too, and the situation would only have grown worse.

Did Zeke mean to alert us, or was something else going on with him that night? Because I don't read minds, either humans' or cats', I won't ever know for sure. But Ann always thought so. She proclaimed him a hero whose timely alarm had likely prevented much greater damage. She thought our builder owed her "watchcat" a big

Christmas present. Zeke didn't get it, but he did get lots of gratitude. And I was glad that despite my reluctance, I had heeded his and Ann's warning.

Years later I was glad that despite my reluctance, I heeded Tom's warning too.

I was a staff writer at an animation studio. Staff writers were assigned to specific shows and worked under story editors. Tom was my boss…and also my mentor and friend. The studio was making staffing cuts, and the show I'd been on was a struggle for me. When it came time to renew my contract for another year, the studio decided to let me go.

I knew the Lord, but my job was such a big part of my life and self-esteem that I felt the world had crashed around my ears. I was in turmoil, but I had one last story to do. Our process was to write an outline first, and then a script. Though I'd only have time to complete an outline before my current contract was up, I was told I could do the script on a freelance basis.

That changed when my boss was reassigned. Our show was ending anyway, and he was moved to a whole new project. I was given a new story editor who had other writers he'd been working with, and now one of them would turn my outline into a script.

My new boss also had different sensibilities than my old boss did. I felt certain that the episode would be totally redone. It seemed quite likely all the work I put in would wind up being scrapped. Emotions roiling, I told Tom I wanted to resign and leave early. Why go through all that effort for nothing? Why put myself through all that pain?

Tom vehemently opposed my plan. I'd been at the studio more than four years. I mustn't quit three weeks from the end. He urged me to stick it out…for myself. I didn't want to heed his warning any more than I wanted to heed Ann and Zeke all those years before. But I knew he was right, and I stayed.

The next three weeks were some of the hardest I had ever known, but I turned in that outline. I finished my race. I learned a lesson in perseverance through that trial, as Scripture says we will. When I made the rounds to say my goodbyes, I could hold my head high. I left on excellent terms with everyone at the studio. And Tom and I had a lovely farewell lunch.

The outline I'd written was effectively scrapped, just as I'd thought it would be. Almost none of my writing remained in the final script. But just as surely as heeding Zeke's and Ann's warning had avoided harm to carpet and vinyl, heeding Tom's had averted damage to my character and reputation.

God also warns us for our good. The prophet Ezekiel, Zeke the cat's namesake, was appointed by God to do this in days of old. The Lord said, "Son of man, I have made you a watchman for the house of Israel; so hear the word I speak and give them warning from me" (Ezekiel 3:17).

Today God warns us through His written Word, His people, and His Spirit. His warnings are meant to spare us grief, like Zeke's and Ann's and Tom's were. So even though it may be tough, choose to hear and heed Him while there is yet time.

Hear, O my people, and I will warn you—if you would but listen to me, O Israel! (Psalm 81:8).

CONSIDER THIS

Have you ever regretted ignoring a warning? Why did you ignore it? What happened as a result? What did you learn that might help you make a wiser choice next time?

Divine CPR

God's Discipline Revives Us

Without discipline, there's no life at all.

Katharine Hepburn

Midnight was a wonderful surprise to us. She was a little black kitten who wandered into our yard and was stranded on our hill. She was there overnight before we caught her. That plus her color was why we named her Midnight. When the veterinarian met her he estimated her age to be four weeks. Somehow she had gotten away from her mother and had managed to survive. Her fur was scruffy, she was very tiny, and she hissed at us over and over out of her fear. Other than being about to starve to death, the doctor said she was healthy.

During the next two years she became the reigning princess of our home. She even looked regal. She was sleek and beautiful with thick soft fur that felt like mink. And it seemed as if she would grant us the favor of petting her, not only for her pleasure, but for ours. She also ruled in our backyard. There she turned from princess to warrior as she terrorized mice, birds, and insects. We took great delight in her. She was thriving in every way. Then one day she suddenly went from the picture of health to being at death's door. She became completely listless and just lay there, not eating or drinking. We quickly rushed her to our veterinarian.

After the doctor checked Midnight out, she asked to keep our kitty, telling us to call the next day for test results. Later that day she phoned to warn us that Midnight might have liver disease. If so, we would probably need to put her down. I was devastated. Tears began to fall like a heavy rain. I completely fell apart. It was as if I had been sitting on a volcano ready to blow, given the right elements, and they all lined up and triggered the eruption. I cried for a full hour before I could even begin to calm down.

Prior to this crisis, I had been struggling with hating my life. My husband had taken early retirement thinking he could get another job, only to discover his advancing age was a put off to prospective employers. He kept looking, but to no avail. I was also finding it hard to watch my children fly the nest. Two were leaving; the other might be soon. I watched their excitement with dismay. Their lives were just starting, and it seemed as if mine was about to finish. And, since we needed more income, we began to take in foreign students. It felt as if my house had the wrong people in it. I was out of control, and I didn't know if I could survive all this.

Looking back, I realize there were many good things in my life at this time. My husband and I still loved each other very much. I had great and close friends. I was in good health. I was involved in ministry in the Christian community. I had cats to amuse and delight me and a yard in which to garden. Above all, I had a strong relationship with my Lord and Savior, Jesus.

These wonderful things, however, were not what I was seeing. I kept concentrating on the things that brought discontentment. Instead of saying, "This is the day the LORD has made; let us rejoice and be glad in it" (Psalm 118:24), my verse would have read, "I don't like the day that the Lord has made, so I'll complain and feel victimized by it."

I felt as if I were being held prisoner. One of my journal entries read, "I realize I am in captivity of sorts. My husband has no job, our son has graduated college and as of yet hasn't been able to find a job, our daughter is about to leave for college, our other son is moving far away, and there are strangers in my home. How do I learn to be content?"

Now, on top of everything else, I might lose Midnight. It was the Friday before Easter, and my church has a Good Friday service not to be missed. Somehow I pulled myself together enough to attend. For the first time in my Christian life, I was deeply in touch with how the disciples must have felt during Jesus' illegal trials and torture and the crucifixion that followed. Of course, my pain was nothing in comparison, but it was real to me, and it left me with feelings of bereavement and confusion, just as the disciples must have experienced on that awful day they saw Jesus die.

As I climbed into bed that night I told the Lord how sorry I was for my months of discontent. I asked Him to help me. My perspective on life had changed. I suddenly knew what was really important. Faced with the prospect of Midnight's death, I realized I had been focusing on the things I didn't like rather than being thankful for the blessings I did have. Nor had I been trusting the Lord to help me with the changes in my life. I was still very sad and teary, but I felt a release after I confessed it all.

The next day the veterinarian called. Midnight didn't have liver disease after all, but an infection, perhaps caused by something she had eaten outdoors. She was rallying after being dosed with intravenous drugs. Those wouldn't have helped if it had been liver disease. Midnight's doctor encouraged us to come in for a visit that day.

My heart hurt to see our little cat hooked up to an IV and curled in a corner of the cage, but I rejoiced to know she would recover. We opened the door and spoke to her, and when she heard my son's voice, she reached her paw toward his hand, touching him. Midnight showed us all how much she loved us as she purred and received our affection. She continued to rally all that day, and was completely well by Easter Sunday.

As I reflected on this event, I was able to see that God used Midnight's severe illness as discipline in my life. He shocked me into putting things in proper perspective. I realized I had been an ungrateful child, concentrating on complaining instead of thanking Him for the blessings I did have. I doubt I would have understood this if Midnight had not been afflicted.

That Easter Sunday was the best Resurrection Sunday I have ever experienced. Just as I had a small taste of the disciples' sorrow over their loss, I had a small taste of their joy and wonder as their loved One was restored to them.

The disciples all knew that Jesus was dead. John had been at the cross and seen Him die. None of them expected to see Him alive in this world again. But suddenly, as they all gathered together that first Easter, there He was, standing in their midst.

I know faith is not a feeling, but feelings can bring deeper dimensions to our faith. Good Friday and Resurrection Sunday have been deeper experiences for me each year since this happened with Midnight.

The first week we brought Midnight home she was in recovery mode, taking drugs that made her very relaxed. I draped her on my shoulders and she stayed there, purring, as I read books or made brownies. It was wonderful. I had my dear little cat again. Not only that, but I began to thank God for my many blessings. Mine was a good life. I had three children who were turning into fine adults. Rather than feeling depressed over that, I began to praise the Lord for who they were. I learned a lot about the power of thanksgiving and praise from the schoolmaster of God's discipline.

I can't say I've never again fallen into discontent, but I am more aware of it when it happens. I am quicker to count my blessings instead of wallowing in self-pity. I am also more aware that I need to take God seriously when He says "give thanks in all circumstances" (1 Thessalonians 5:18).

My husband never found another job, but he generates income in other ways. We still house foreign students, but now I realize God has sent them to us for His purposes. I still miss my children living at home, but I know their leaving is within His purpose too.

The Bible says God disciplines those whom He loves (Hebrews 12:6). Though it's no fun while it's going on, discipline brings good and godly results, and it is proof that we are His and that He cares for us.

Our fathers disciplined us for a little while as they thought best; but God disciplines us for our good, that we may share in his holiness. No discipline seems pleasant at the time, but painful. Later on, however, it produces a harvest of righteousness and peace for those who have been trained by it (Hebrews 12:10-11).

CONSIDER THIS

Is there an area of your life where God is disciplining you? What about it is painful? What might God be trying to teach you?

Are you praising and thanking God in all circumstances? If not, how might you begin to do so?

Hollow Paw Syndrome and Its Cure

Fill Up on God

You say, "If I had a little more, I should be very satisfied." You make a mistake. If you are not content with what you have, you would not be satisfied if it were doubled.

Charles Haddon Spurgeon

Have you ever heard the expression, "He (or she) has a hollow leg?" It's often applied to active teens in a growth spurt. They have a ravenous appetite and consume vast quantities of food while managing to retain the figure of an oversized toothpick.

Well, my cat Barney got a "hollow paw"...not in his youth, but in his old age. In the case of my cat, it was due not to healthy growth, but to metabolic malfunction.

I was feeding Barney what I always had, but he was losing weight and clamoring for extra wet food, which he much prefers to kibble. The vet checked for diabetes, but my cat didn't have it. She probed further and discovered his thyroid was slightly overactive. He's now on medication and it seems to be working.

I could have fed Barney more, but it wouldn't have handled the underlying cause of his overactive appetite. Feeding me more money didn't handle the underlying cause of my overactive appetite, either, when I "shopped till I dropped" on a college tour to Europe.

I was 18 years old and had just completed my freshman year of college. This was my first-ever trip overseas. My parents had gone there a number of times and had brought back some wonderful purchases. Now I could make my own. I was salivating.

I traveled on a tour with 23 other students, a professor, and a guide. We went to 12 countries in 6 weeks. We had great fun, saw famous art history landmarks...and shopped. I bought wood carvings in Germany, crystal in Czechoslovakia, gold and turquoise jewelry in Istanbul's Grand Bazaar—and the list goes on. As I recall, Mom and Dad had given me $500 in spending money—no paltry sum back in 1966. I went through all my traveler's checks and called home for more funds...which they wired.

Our tour ended in Paris. I was flying on to London with two friends from the trip. Other kids from our group were headed there too. By this time, I'd made so many purchases that my bags were literally spilling over. One of the guys had bought some things that wouldn't even fit in his luggage...a World War I Prussian army helmet and an antique Turkish sword. I vaguely remember he carried the sword and wore the helmet on his head as we staggered with our bloated baggage toward some eye-rolling British customs officials.

The customs officials knew when to yell "uncle"—as in Uncle Sam. They chuckled that we were Americans...we had to be with a rig like that. They waved us through without searching our bags... probably realizing that if they opened our luggage they might never get it closed again.

You'd have thought I'd quit shopping. No way! I had nine days in London and Scotland before I would fly to Copenhagen to join my parents. They were meeting me for three more weeks of travel to wind up my European summer. I was running short of funds... but how could I pass up purchases in two new countries? I threw prudence to the winds and bought more. The last thing I got was a sweater in Scotland. By the time I boarded the flight for Denmark, I was just a few dollars from broke. But hey, my parents were just a flight away.

My parents were livid!

It wasn't the overspending that distressed my dad the most. I had left myself virtually no cash for emergencies. He saw a deeper problem, a lack of wisdom and self-control that would not be fixed by feeding me more money.

Dad zipped his wallet and gave me a dose of reality. He pointed out how foolish I'd been. He made me consider what might have happened had I gotten into trouble with no funds to bail myself out. And he pointed out what I had missed by not conserving my cash—lovely things I saw while traveling with my parents that I had no money left to buy. Dad relented and bought me a small Danish porcelain desert fox I still have to this day. But he mostly let me take the consequences of my actions. Even though his medicine was hard to swallow, it taught me a big lesson.

But even Dad's medicine failed to address a still deeper cause of my hunger for things. I was seeking satisfaction that can only be found in God. Later in my college career, I asked Jesus to come into my heart, forgive my sins, and be my Savior and Lord. As I have grown and matured in my faith, I've learned that I often use food or possessions to meet needs that only God can fill. God has given me these things to enjoy, but when my appetite for them spirals out of control, as it still does, it usually signals an underlying spiritual metabolic malfunction. Larger helpings of earthly things can't heal that. Only God can.

Barney's a cat. He just knows he's hungry. He doesn't understand why. He meows for food and eats what I put in front of him. But

I'm God's child. I have insight, and I can make choices. I can try to satisfy hollow paw syndrome by stuffing myself with the things of this world and find myself hungry again a little while later. Or I can feast on God and His Word and be filled up forever.

Jesus answered, "Everyone who drinks this water will be thirsty again, but whoever drinks the water I give him will never thirst. Indeed, the water I give him will become in him a spring of water welling up to eternal life" (John 4:13-14).

CONSIDER THIS

What earthly things have you hungered for? Is your appetite for them excessive? If so, what deeper need might be behind this? How might God satisfy it?

If Cats Could Talk

Insight Breeds Compassion

If you do not understand a man you cannot crush him. And if you do understand him, very probably you will not.

Gilbert K. Chesterton

I'm a person who hates being nagged. Something in me rebels when I feel badgered—even by my cats. And I was definitely feeling hounded by Barney. He'd always been a talker, but he'd ramped his meowing way up of late, and it was becoming a major pet peeve of mine.

My cats hang out in the kitchen/den area of my home. I'd be working in my office and go down for lunch or dinner. When Barney saw me, he'd leave his corner or perch and follow me, yowling.

I'm a writer who works at home. Meal breaks are important to me. Sometimes I keep chewing on a story as I eat my food. Other days, I just feel a need to unwind. I either lose myself in thought or read unrelated material for diversion. An incessantly mewing cat is not an intrusion that furthers these ends—and it scrapes like fingernails on the chalkboard of my nervous system. Barney's yowling made me want to scream. If the onslaught didn't stop, I either fled or banished him. Selfishly, I just wanted the noise to cease. I became increasingly irritated with my poor kitty.

Barney didn't mew just at me. Friends got a dose of it too. One pal suggested Barney might be having trouble reaching his food. Old and stiff, he was struggling to spring to the counter where I kept the cats' food so my dogs wouldn't eat it. I started lifting him to his dinner, and it helped a little, but it didn't make the problem go away.

Cats can't talk. Poor Barney couldn't tell me what was bothering him. So it fell to my vet to shed greater light on his behavior. As I mentioned in the previous story, my vet discovered a medical problem that increased Barney's appetite. He was probably lobbying for more food. Another possible cause of the howling was senility.

Barney's noisiness still irritates me, especially when my nerves are frayed. But it does help to know why he's doing what he's doing. Knowing why my mother does what she does has also helped me deal with a bothersome behavior of hers.

From childhood my pet peeve with my mom was her constant insistence that she was right. It meant that whenever we differed, I was always wrong. This drove me nuts. It probably made me feel diminished. I saw it as arrogance on her part. When I grew up, I tried to avoid acting like this with others. I told friends, "Take my words with a grain of salt. Think about what I've said and draw your own conclusions. I could be in error." I was drawn to people who acknowledged mistakes. I was put off by those who stayed stuck on their positions.

And then Mom became very ill. God let me know I was to love her just as she was. I surrendered my will and committed to do so, in His power. It transformed our relationship. We began to talk. One day, we discussed Mom's need to be right. She offered an insight that turned my irritation on its ear. She said she thought she needed to be right because when she was a child, her stepmother had always made her wrong.

I still become irritated at Mom when she gets stuck on her position, but I will never view her the same way I once did. I now see this as an expression of her pain. I can imagine her as a young child, crumbling inside as her thoughts and opinions were cut down time after time. I have a compassion I didn't before—and it has colored my response to this behavior and always will.

Mom's revelation reminded me of something I first realized years ago when I was a very young Christian. Much of what we humans do that is hurtful or dysfunctional stems from our own brokenness. I can't always know why people act the way they do. But God knows—and His Spirit indwells me. I have the mind of Christ. I can pray for His insight. I can ask Him to help me see others through "Christ-colored glasses."

Understanding may not always banish irritation with pets or people, but it can certainly give it pause. It breeds compassion, which brings healing to us as well as others. So next time you're tempted to grit your teeth, why not get on your knees and pray instead—and see what God may do?

God gave Solomon wisdom and very great insight, and a breadth of understanding as measureless as the sand on the seashore (1 Kings 4:29).

CONSIDER THIS

Do you have a pet peeve about someone that has irritated you? How has it affected your feelings and behavior toward that person? Have you asked God to give you His insight about it? If so, what effect has that had?

Part IV

Scratching Post Guidance

God Teaches Us His Ways

PUMPKIN & MIDNIGHT

Follow That Pumpkin

Seek Spiritual Role Models

Imitation is the sincerest of flattery.

Charles Caleb Colton

I heard her first, while I was reading in my yard on a hot September afternoon: "Mew, mew, mew." From the sound I guessed it was a kitten. My son came outside, and it was he who spotted her. All we could see were bright green eyes because she was black, and it was dark in the shrubbery.

We finally caught the tiny kitten. Her fur was matted, and she looked like an old stuffed toy ready for the trash. We thought she was about four weeks old. We watched as she gulped down the food we gave her and guessed that she was starving. Our vet confirmed this but said otherwise she seemed healthy. We named the orphan Midnight and welcomed her into our loving, cat-friendly home.

Midnight had no mother to show her how to be a cat. But we had three cats already, so she picked a new mom from among them. Her choice was Pumpkin, our male orange tabby.

Pumpkin wasn't sure he wanted the job of mentoring a tiny kitten, so he tried to run from his new responsibility. Although one-fourth his size, Midnight wasn't shy about following him. We'd watch Pumpkin tearing furiously through the house with a little black streak close on his paws. If he stopped, she stopped. If he raced, she raced. It was like seeing taillights flashing by on a freeway, but the colors were orange and black. Eventually Pumpkin learned to escape by jumping onto high counters that Midnight couldn't yet reach, but for those first few weeks he could no more get rid of her than he could shake his own shadow.

Midnight patterned herself after Pumpkin. If he passed her sleeping form on the way to his food dish, she bolted awake and trailed him there. Then she took a few bites of her food just because he was having some of his. He had become her role model. She wanted to imitate everything he did.

At first we didn't let Midnight follow Pumpkin outside. She would sit by the door awaiting his return. He'd come in for a catnap, and she'd crawl up on a nearby chair to watch him doze off and then inch closer so she could sleep touching him. Once I was resting on the sofa with Pumpkin on my lap, and Midnight suddenly joined us, climbing from my shoulders to my chest and curling up near where he was.

Midnight even learned to spray the bushes because of Pumpkin. She watched him turn his tail around and let go, and she imitated that too. She was female, but that didn't stop her. It's the one thing I wish she hadn't learned from him because she started spraying in the house!

Pumpkin's influence on Midnight's personality and behavior helped make her the wonderful ten-year-old kitty she is today. You could say he helped mold her life as a cat.

Dotty Larson was my spiritual mother, and she was instrumental in molding my life as a child of God.

Dotty taught a Bible study class of 600 women. I had joined the class at the urging of a friend. From the first time I heard her, I loved her teaching. She made the Bible come alive. She brought in history and culture. She used humor. She was scholarly, and yet her teaching was also practical. One day she said, "If you've never asked Jesus to take over your life before this, why not do it now?" That day I invited Him to be my Lord.

Dotty didn't know me personally at that time, but I got to know her well from her lectures. When she explained that Jesus had washed away all of our sins, I felt warm, as if wrapped in a blanket. I loved that she was sold out to Jesus. I loved how she brought Bible stories to life. Her faith was something I wanted to emulate. I could hardly wait for class. It was the highlight of my week.

She became my role model. Her example taught me how to go to the Lord at each moment of my own life, how to walk in righteousness, and how to pray. She was honest, so nothing got pushed aside. She shared her own struggles. She shared how she wrestled with certain passages of Scripture and with the troubles of this life. She would say, "We can't understand it all, but we can trust the One who does." Her faith wasn't shallow; it ran deep, and it defined her. Her dedication and the way she walked with Jesus in the power of the Spirit made me want to be exactly like her. If I could have, I would have followed her everywhere, just as Midnight had shadowed Pumpkin.

To my amazement and delight, I did get the chance to grow closer to Dotty. In time, I was asked to join the class's leadership team. Now I could follow and learn from her not at a distance, but in a close, intimate group. We were nicknamed "Big Dotty and Little Dottie" because I was 20 years her junior and I also had been given the gift of teaching. She sensed the gift in me before I did. She let me give devotionals, and then one day she invited me to take a lecture for her. Afterward she sat with me. "You have the gift too. It will be both a burden and a joy to you," she said.

Dotty's influence helped shape the way I teach my own Bible class today. She played the role Paul described when he said, "I urge you to imitate me" (1 Corinthians 4:16). She was worthy of imitation because she always pointed to Christ.

I was blessed with Dotty Larson as a wonderful role model of a woman who took God seriously. I learned to take Him seriously too by following her example. And it has changed my life forever... just as following Pumpkin changed Midnight.

Remember your leaders, who spoke the word of God to you. Consider the outcome of their way of life and imitate their faith (Hebrews 13:7).

CONSIDER THIS

If you are a young believer, do you have a spiritual mentor? If so, what are you learning from that person? If not, have you prayed for a spiritual role model?

If you are a more mature Christian, are you walking with the Lord in a way that could be an example to others? Who might God be calling you to mentor in the faith?

A Cat in Doll's Clothing

Be Who God Made You

Always be a first-rate version of yourself, instead of a second-rate version of somebody else.

Judy Garland

When I was a child I had a doll named Madeline. She came clothed in a lovely red-and-white dress. That dress was specially made for this doll. It fit her perfectly.

It did not fit Fluffy.

Fluffy was part of a litter of kittens born on my family's back porch. She came dressed in a beautiful gray-and-white fur coat. Not only did it fit her perfectly, it actually grew with her. It totally met her wardrobe needs and allowed complete freedom of movement. Like my doll's maker, my cat's Creator had designed this one-of-a-kind garment just for her. But one day I decided to improve on the situation.

The notion to play dress up with my cat was probably inspired by Mom. She loved pictures of kitties decked out in human clothing. But when I put Madeline's dress on Fluffy, my pet was less than amused. It just wasn't made for an animal that runs on all fours. It hog-tied that cat. After snapping a picture of my miserable feline looking less than pleased in her new attire, I mercifully released her from her cloth prison.

I'm sure if Fluffy knew human speech, she would have given me a talking-to. She would have said, "Silly human, what were you thinking? I'm not some two-dimensional greeting card or postcard kitty. I'm a real cat. And real cats don't wear puffed sleeves!"

Looking back, I can smile at my efforts to stuff Fluffy into that ill-fitting garment. But I've realized I've done the same thing to myself. I've tried to stuff myself into other people's personalities or talents, and they haven't fit me any better than that dress fit Fluffy.

One such ill-fitting identity was a "fantasy dress" I modeled all alone in my room as a kid. It represented a longing to be popular. I fancied myself a famous young singer who had audiences wowed. I'd put a record on my stereo and jump around in my bedroom, pretending it was my voice singing. I even made up a new name for myself. But I didn't have much of a singing voice. I wasn't some bubbly, outgoing star. This wasn't a dress I could wear in public. And though it was relatively harmless, spending hours in my head being someone else didn't help me learn to be the person my Creator designed me to be.

In college I gave my life to Christ. As I grew in my faith, I learned that God made me special. I learned I was His unique creation. I learned He doesn't make mistakes. I learned that...but I didn't quite believe it. As I looked around me, it seemed there were others who had more attractive dresses than I did and got more love and attention as a result. I coveted one friend's stunning good looks. I longed for another's life-of-the-party personality.

And then someone I was sharing this with made a comment I'll never forget. That confidante said if I'd be myself, I'd attract the friends I was supposed to have. They'd be the friends who were right for me because they'd be drawn to the real me, not some person I was trying to be that I wasn't.

Those words burrowed deep inside my soul. Over time I have learned they are true. One thing that has helped is discovering my spiritual gifts. I'd long been aware that I had a gift of mercy. When I joined a Bible study class and was invited into leadership, I discovered I had gifts of shepherding and encouragement too. As I began to give these gifts, I developed rich, meaningful relationships with people who sought me out for who I really am.

In the fashion world, the most coveted garments are those that are one of a kind. People pay huge sums for designer haute couture gowns, each of which is completely unique and tailored to be an exact fit for the wearer. If I had such a gown, would I alter it to copy another? Of course not!

These days, I want my inner gown to be an original too. I no longer wish to scrunch myself into Fluffy's dress. I want to revel in the one-of-a-kind person God made me to be, and model His creation for His glory forever.

We are God's masterpiece. He has created us anew in Christ Jesus, so we can do the good things he planned for us long ago (Ephesians 2:10 NLT).

CONSIDER THIS

Have you ever tried to dress yourself in someone else's personality or talents? What was the result? What special gifts and talents has God given you? If you're not sure, who might help you find out? How might you use your gifts for God's glory?

A Time to Work

Diligence Is Next to Godliness

A man who gives his children habits of industry provides for them better than by giving them fortune.

Richard Whately

We've had two kinds of cats during our marriage—fluffy, lazy house cats and hardworking farm cats. Our very first feline, Kelly, was the former kind. She was a beautiful calico who seemed to have only one goal in life—finding the most comfortable spot in the house where she could sleep the day away. When we came home in the evening, we would often need to lift her off our easy chair or sofa. She also loved to curl up on a pile of clean laundry that hadn't been folded and put away.

One day we heard an awful cat sound coming from somewhere near the back of our little home. We searched everywhere for her, without success. All at once we looked at each other, gasped, and ran to the clothes dryer. We pulled it open and there she sat, looking quite dizzy. Miraculously, she was none the worse for her spin. The consequences could have been dire. We were careful to make sure that didn't happen again, but she kept curling up and sleeping comfortably in any other place she could find. Her only goal was her comfort.

In contrast, Kitty was a hardworking farm cat. Though she lived in the house for a while, she seemed to feel her place was outside. When she had kittens, she kept them outdoors and taught them to hunt. We fed them too, but they enjoyed catching small prey for their food and kept down the rodent numbers in our yard. We were grateful.

When we had children, we didn't want them to be fluffy and lazy, like Kelly. We wanted them to be hardworking like Kitty. We knew we had to train them this way, just as Kitty had trained her kittens.

We didn't order our three kids to work on the farm, but if they wanted extra money, that was one way to get it. We started them at about age 12, chopping weeds out of young cotton plants. As they grew older, their duties grew larger. They learned to drive the farm pick-ups—which gave them a big head start when it came time to take driver's education at school. They all learned to drive tractors too.

Our son, John, began repairing motors before he was 13. This inspired him to go to auto tech school later on. Now he has a well-paying job as an auto mechanic and excels in his field. Our younger daughter Karen has worked on her '57 Chevy Bel Air for years and knows more about cars than many young men. Our older daughter Christy carried her work ethic over into music and teaching. My husband, Steve, and I taught all three of our children to work with excellence and diligence, and they do so to this day. This is pleasing to us, and we're proud of each one.

Even more important than pleasing us, our children have learned that doing their best is pleasing to God. Whether it's hoeing weeds, fixing cars, running a business, or caring for people, God wants them to do their work unto Him—even in a less than ideal job situation.

Christy's first classroom teaching position was not at all in her comfort zone. She was hired as a long-term substitute teacher just a few weeks after school started. She had all the responsibilities of a full-time teacher, but the pay was much less. This situation was not her preference, but she stayed there and gave her all to teach those children for the rest of the school year. She didn't do less work for less pay—she did her best for the Lord. Rather than whining and complaining about it, she said the experience of this school would help her anywhere else she might go.

It's only fitting that we do our best work for God. He did His best work for us. He made this marvelous creation. He made man in His own image. He made woman so man wouldn't be alone. And when they ate the forbidden fruit and marred His perfect workmanship with sin, God didn't throw in the towel on this less than ideal situation. He did an even greater work. He sent His own Son to die for us, that we and all creation might be redeemed. And He continues even now to work in those who've received this gift of salvation. Scripture tells us, "Continue to work out your salvation with fear and trembling, for it is God who works in you to will and to act according to his good purpose" (Philippians 2:12-13).

If God works with such excellence and diligence on our behalf, can we not do so also, to please Him and glorify His name?

Whatever you do, work at it with all your heart, as working for the Lord, not for men, since you know that you will receive an inheritance from the Lord as a reward. It is the Lord Christ you are serving (Colossians 3:23-24).

CONSIDER THIS

Have you ever been in a less than ideal work situation? How did you handle it? What were the results? How did this reflect on your witness for the Lord? How might you be more diligent and excellent in your work right now?

Of Claws and Covenants

Keep Your Word, As God Does

God never made a promise that
was too good to be true.

Dwight L. Moody

Muffin's breeder was adamant. I had to promise not to declaw her. If I trained her right, she would scratch on her scratching posts, not my furniture. I knew many shared the breeder's concerns about the potential ill effects of declawing. And I'd fallen in love with this Ragdoll kitten. So I gave my word.

Muffin didn't give hers.

It wasn't the furniture she went for. It was the grass-cloth wallpaper. Its nubby texture seemed to scream "scratch on me" to a feline. It covered the walls in the downstairs area where I kept my cats. Muffin soon picked a favorite spot to scratch. If I caught her, I stopped her, but I wasn't always there to do that, and I didn't like the results of her efforts one bit!

Okay, so Muffin's transgressions were partly my fault. I bought scratching posts, but I didn't work with her on using them. Still, I was tempted to break my word to that breeder. It would solve my wallpaper problem, right? And the breeder wouldn't ever have to know.

Of course, there was the ethical dilemma of causing my cat pain to preserve my home decor. But even without that, I couldn't break my promise. To do so would have scratched up my integrity...which I valued far more than wall covering. I had made a covenant with that breeder, and it didn't depend on what Muffin did. It depended on who I was.

So did my promise to my parents about baptism, and I think that's one reason why God made sure I kept my word about that too.

I am a Jewish believer in Jesus. As a child I'd been intrigued with the deep Christian faith of some people I greatly admired. I'd also decided that being born into a particular belief system wasn't, in itself, reason enough to embrace it. I started to search for God on my own, exploring other faiths and philosophies. But it was the Christian faith that most strongly drew me.

When it came time for college, I chose a small liberal arts school that happened to have a loose Christian affiliation. I studied religion as part of a mandatory course on the history of Western civilization. I joined the choir and sang in chapel. Midway through my freshman year of college, I was thinking about being baptized.

I didn't yet believe that Jesus was God, but I thought He was a great man and teacher. I asked our college chaplain if I could be baptized on that basis. He urged me to speak with a local pastor, who told me that wouldn't be appropriate. To take that step, I needed to believe in the divinity of Christ. We started meeting weekly to talk more about the biblical evidence for this. Meanwhile I had told my parents what I was considering.

I still recall one particular phone call with my mom and dad. They didn't try to stop me from searching, but they made a request. They asked that I not get baptized till I turned 21. I agreed. I was then 18.

Not two years later, at a different school, after being presented with Old Testament prophesies about the Messiah, I asked Jesus to forgive my sins and come into my heart. I put my faith in Him as Messiah, Savior, and Lord. I could now be baptized, and in fact the Bible commanded me to do so as a witness to my faith. But…I wasn't 21 yet. And I had made a promise.

My parents needn't have known I got baptized any more than Muffin's breeder need have known I'd declawed her, if I'd chosen to do that. But I felt an inner nudge to keep my word and wait. I'd also heard some conflicting views about what baptism meant. The extra time let me settle this in my heart. I turned 21. A few months later, I was baptized with a small group of others—joyfully and with a clear conscience.

One reason I kept my word to my parents was probably the ethics they'd instilled in me. They believed in the Ten Commandments. They had biblical standards of morality. They taught me that a decent, upright person does what he or she says. But as I've grown in my faith, I've discovered an even more compelling reason. God wants His children to reflect who He is, to do what He does. And He never, ever breaks His promises.

Abraham knew this. He believed God's promise to make him the father of a great nation even when God asked him to sacrifice his son Isaac (Genesis 22). Abraham bound the lad on the altar, trusting God would somehow keep His word. God did not disappoint. He stayed Abraham's hand and provided a ram to die in Isaac's place.

God provided a Lamb to die in my place…Jesus, the Lamb of God. He did so because I'm not perfect and I mess up. I don't keep my word every single time, but Jesus paid for that. Through faith in Christ, I've become God's child. All His promises are for me. He isn't pleased when I scratch on the grass cloth, but He'll keep His word to me nonetheless. And when I keep mine, I reflect and honor Him.

God is not a man, that he should lie, nor a son of man, that he should change his mind. Does he speak and then not act? Does he promise and not fulfill? (Numbers 23:19).

CONSIDER THIS

When was the last time someone broke a promise to you? What happened? How did it make you feel? How did it affect your relationship with that person?

Which of God's promises is most precious to you, and why?

Unwelcome Offerings

Give Gifts That Please God

The excellence of a gift lies in its appropriateness rather than in its value.

Charles Dudley Warner

There's a mouse in my house! Right now, as I write this, I know there is an uninvited rodent hiding somewhere in my home. I was sitting alone, reading in the living room two nights ago, when I saw it scurry across the floor to hide in a new location. We've hunted for it ever since. Eventually we will find it and evict it.

The reason for this uninvited guest is our black cat, Midnight.

We call Midnight the mouse world's worst nightmare. She loves to hunt all sorts of prey in our large and rather wild backyard. Midnight excels in her skill. We've watched her spot a mouse or bird and take off in the opposite direction so she can circle around through the underbrush and catch it off guard. All our other cats have gone in a straight line toward their prey, which usually means they have ended up empty pawed.

Midnight is always proud of her catch, so she brings whatever it is to her favorite humans, no doubt as a trophy of love. In her cat mind, she seems to think we'll be thrilled with these offerings. I can't remember being thrilled even once. Disgusted? Alarmed? Troubled? Yes! Thrilled? Not ever.

I've fled out the back door when she has marched proudly through the cat door carrying a mouse. I screamed the day she brought in a bird, and when I did, thankfully she let it go. We opened all the doors and the happy bird found its way back to freedom. Another day I heard a strange buzzing noise I couldn't figure out. Then I saw her pounce on a scarab beetle near where I was sitting. She had brought it inside too. This began a series of beetle sightings that left us mystified as to whether Midnight brought in one scarab beetle fifteen different times, or fifteen different beetles, one time each.

My worst response to her offerings was to a potato bug. If you've ever seen one, you'll empathize with my reaction. I let out a bloodcurdling scream the moment I laid eyes on it. My teenaged children heard the shriek and raced downstairs to save me from whatever intruder was trying to kill me. When they realized it was not a would-be murderer but a nasty-looking insect, they were angry about the false alarm for an entire week.

That bug may have been the worst of my unwanted presents from my cat, but it certainly wasn't the last. If it was out there, she'd find it. If the cat door was open, she'd bring it in and lay it at our feet. When I saw the aforementioned mouse, I groaned to her, "Why do you keep bringing me gifts I don't want?" Suddenly I began to think of things I bring to God that He doesn't want. One such offering was trying to help God with my husband's spiritual condition.

Phil and I were not believers when we married each other. When I came to know Jesus I wanted him to have Jesus too. I began to tell Phil how much he needed the Lord. For some strange reason, he didn't agree. So I kept trying to persuade him…over and over and over. I thought I was helping God by doing this. After all, we must be bold witnesses, right? But the more I pushed my point, the more resistance I encountered. Proverbs 27:15 says, "A quarrelsome wife is like a constant dripping on a rainy day." That was who I was. I talked too much and loved too little.

Phil later said that he knew I wanted to persuade him, but it felt more as if I were nagging him about something I needed him to do rather than having a genuine desire for him to know God. It did nothing to develop his own longing for the Lord.

Even though I thought I was pleasing God, I was bringing Him the wrong gift. He must have felt the way I do when Midnight brings me her unwelcome offerings. I needed to learn to discern what God wanted, as David did when he wrote, "You do not delight in sacrifice, or I would bring it; you do not take pleasure in burnt offerings. The sacrifices of God are a broken spirit; a broken and contrite heart, O God, you will not despise" (Psalm 51:16-17).

It wasn't long before I began to hear messages about how a believing wife is to treat her unbelieving husband. I love the way God brings the exact words we need to hear when we are acting in ignorance. I heard one preacher say wives should talk to God about their husbands rather than to their husbands about God. I heard another person on the radio share that what brought her husband to Jesus was when she shut up and just loved him for who he was. Later I would study 1 Peter and learn the truth of the admonition, "You wives, be submissive to your own husbands, so that even if any of them are disobedient to the word, they may be won without a word by the behavior of their wives" (1 Peter 3:1 NASB).

I began to pay more attention to my life with Jesus than to Phil's life without Him. That was a good thing for both of us, and it brought happiness back to our home. I also began to love Phil the way God wanted, with a quiet and submissive spirit. I learned to be silent about Jesus and let my life be the witness God intended it to be.

I began to understand that no one can talk another person into God's kingdom. We can witness to others about our lives and we can live that witness in front of them, but we can't be the Holy Spirit to them. Once I stopped bringing offerings to the Lord that were not pleasing to Him, He began to work in my husband. My badgering had been to Phil what Midnight's mice had been to me...something he couldn't stand. Once the nagging was gone, he began to respond to God's wooing. Phil is a Christian now, and I can humbly say my words had nothing to do with it. I have learned a lot about witnessing for the Lord since that time, and I have found the best testimony is when I am walking in ways that please Him.

I'm glad to say Midnight's mouse is gone too since the time I began this story. We left the back door open one evening, and it scurried outside. We have now closed the cat door permanently to avoid any more such presents. Being a kitty, Midnight can't understand what's acceptable to us. But as God's people, we can learn what pleases Him and bring Him the offerings He desires.

Live as children of light (for the fruit of the light consists in all goodness, righteousness and truth) and find out what pleases the Lord (Ephesians 5:8-10).

CONSIDER THIS

Have you ever given God an unwelcome offering? What was it? What happened as a result? How did you discover what God really wanted? What changed when you gave Him the gift He desired?

Baby Steps

Spiritual Milk Before Meat

Step by step is the law of growth. God does not expect the acorn to be a mighty oak before it has become a sapling.

George E. Carpenter

Wally was so tiny you could say she was a condensed version of a kitty. She was born on our roof and fell through a hole into an entry wall of our home when her mama was moving her kittens into our attic. It took a lot to get Wally out, but we managed. When we held her, we all fell in love with her.

Besides being tiny, Wally was skinny. Probably because she wasn't eating, her mama gave her up for dead. But we didn't. My daughters, Christy and Karen, called our vet for advice. They were told to feed her special preemie formula through a preemie feeding tube, much like an eyedropper.

Special care for Wally began. She had a pretty little pink blanket to sleep on. Every four hours, the girls prepared her formula. Then one of us would hold and feed Wally—not out of duty, but of love. We all took turns, but Christy and Karen were in charge.

When the preemie food was finished, it was time to give Wally kitten food. The girls put a small amount on a dish and set it on the kitchen floor. Then they put Wally down beside it and encouraged her to eat it. Once she realized what it was, she gobbled it on her own. As she grew older, she graduated to regular cat food. Though she never became big, she grew into a nice healthy kitty.

Karen was tiny when she was born too. She was six weeks premature. Like Wally, she required special care. She had jaundice, which had to be treated by keeping her in an incubator with a special light. She didn't know how to suck, so I had to put my milk in a special little bottle with a tiny nipple. I held her little body and the bottle, and wrapped my fingers around her mouth, manipulating her lips and mouth to suck. Getting her to drink two ounces was a magnificent feat, but she eventually figured it out. When she did, she was ready to take my milk in the normal way.

In the beginning, Karen's voice was as tiny as her size. She would sound a petite whimper about every four hours. We'd pick her up, change her, feed her, and put her back to sleep again. Sometimes we'd have to wake her up to eat. But as she grew, her voice did too. Soon she was sounding a lusty yell when she needed something or she was hungry. By the time she was two, she was helping herself from our refrigerator. Now she's all grown up and puts healthy adult food into her 24-year-old body.

Just as Wally and Karen needed milk before they could manage solid food, we need milk before meat when learning about God's Word. When I went to Sunday school as a child, I learned about Jesus by hearing Bible stories told in a way that I could understand. We also learned special songs that helped the Bible come alive. I sang about the wee little man Zacchaeus who climbed up into a sycamore tree to see the Lord. I loved the song because I could relate to a small person wanting to see Jesus. I often thought how wonderful it would be to climb a tree and talk to Him. He would come to my tree and tell me that He was coming to my house today.

Spiritually speaking, we all need to start with baby food, like Wally. And like Karen, some of us even need to learn to suck on the bottle. But if we are nurtured in this way, we'll grow healthy and strong and be able to thrive on adult food later—just as they did.

Like newborn babies, crave pure spiritual milk, so that by it you may grow up in your salvation, now that you have tasted that the Lord is good (1 Peter 2:2-3).

CONSIDER THIS

Have you been nurtured on spiritual milk in your Christian life? If not, how might you get some? If so, how did it help you? How might you help others get the pure milk of God's Word?

Kitty Learning Curves

Sometimes We Must Learn the Hard Way

The only real mistake is the one
from which we learn nothing.

John Powell

Merlin was a beautiful male orange tabby I adopted from a cat rescue group. He'd been hit by a car and still had a slight limp when I got him. His foster mom warned me not to let him overtax his leg. Too bad she didn't tell it to him—not that he would have listened, even if he could have understood her.

"Big Red" clearly had a strong macho streak. If his leg was gimpy, his aspirations weren't. He wasn't content just to climb and leap with his kitty peers. He wanted more. He tried to become the Evel Knievel of felines.

I had a double oven in my kitchen with a cabinet above it. My other male cat, Barney, was much younger then. He liked to curl up on the cabinet's top. He'd spring to the counter beside the oven, then launch himself airborne to that favorite perch, seven feet above the ground. Merlin wanted to get there too...but he had a different route in mind. He'd already been jumping from another counter to the top of my refrigerator. One day I caught him poised on the fridge's edge, eyeing Barney's cabinet perch. I realized he wanted to leap to it across a chasm of kitchen floor. I doubted he'd make it. I waved him off.

He didn't stay waved off.

Perhaps I should have tried harder to stop him, but after a few attempts to do so, I felt he was bound to take the leap sometime. I couldn't police him 24 hours a day. And I reasoned it might be better to be present when he took the plunge. So the next time he seemed poised to try kitty Olympics, I just waited and watched. He crouched. He sprang. He almost made it before splatting down on the kitchen floor. He scrambled up and sauntered off, and to my knowledge he never tried that feat again.

Taking that fall taught Merlin a lesson I sensed he might not learn otherwise. Sometimes God has had to let me learn the hard way too. One area where this has been true is my lifelong struggle with my weight. Sadly, I haven't had as quick a learning curve as my cat.

I started getting chunky around puberty. Even then, I was the sedentary type. I had a slightly gimpy metabolism too. I envied friends who could chow down and still perch on the cabinet of thinness. I eyed them from my fridge of plumpness till at last I decided to leap the chasm between us by dieting.

Unlike Merlin, I made it...but just barely. I wasn't curled up on the cabinet, I was dangling precariously by my paws. I starved and binged. I exercised compulsively. I was suffering from a borderline eating disorder and about to take a fall that would jeopardize my health and perhaps my life.

My dad saw the danger and stepped in. He helped me stabilize my weight and eat a balanced diet in my senior year of high school. But I didn't get well in my head. My weight bounced up and down in college and remained an obsession. I felt so tortured I reached out for God...and that was good. But I wouldn't get off what became a lifelong roller coaster ride of gaining and losing.

No matter how hard my loved ones and God tried to wave me off, I wouldn't hear them.

I didn't get back into the kind of danger I had in high school. Still, I was leaping for a perch that didn't suit me. I was trying to be too thin for my build and metabolism. When the effort required to sustain this became too much, I took yet another fall...and another...and another.

Merlin learned his lesson on his first tumble. Learning mine took more than 40 years. But at last I'm hoping my splats on the floor are over. Last year I joined a weight management program that provides group support and promotes healthy lifestyle changes. I accepted that being who God made me was the best me to be. I listened to my loved ones and set a healthy, realistic weight goal. I've now reached that new perch, and it feels great!

Obeying God sooner would have spared me a lot of pain and grief. But I've grown on the journey, and it has taught me things. I've learned I can't force myself into a mold that doesn't fit me and sustain it. And I've realized that what matters most to my friends and loved ones isn't who I am outside. It's who I am inside that draws them.

I made the best choice I knew for Merlin...but I couldn't be certain of the outcome. I couldn't guarantee that his tumble would work for his good. In retrospect, perhaps I let him take an undue risk. Perhaps I should have tried harder to find a way to stop him. I'm not all-powerful or all-knowing. God is. He knows the lessons I need to learn. He knows what it will take to teach me. And even when I drag out my learning curve, He can use my missteps for my good, to grow and mature me in Him.

Before I was afflicted I went astray, but now I obey your word…It was good for me to be afflicted so that I might learn your decrees (Psalm 119:67,71).

CONSIDER THIS

Has there been a lesson God tried to teach you that you resisted learning? What was it? Why did you drag out your learning curve? What were the results? How did God use your missteps to grow you?

Moving Day

When Life Changes, God Doesn't

Change is not made without inconvenience, even from worse to better.

Richard Hooker

There he was, sleeping contentedly on my belly. I had just awakened from a short nap on the sofa on this cold, rainy day. I had to stay on my back because of an inner ear problem, and Mooch had taken full advantage of the nice warm spot he'd found. As I stirred, he opened his eyes and blinked them in happy recognition. *My, how far he has come,* I thought. *He's starting to feel at home.*

Mooch had come to us from another family. This change had been thrust upon him. Everything was different from what he had known in his previous four years.

I've heard it said that the one constant thing in life is change. In one brief moment something can shift and life becomes radically different. This was true for Mooch. It also happened to a dear friend I'll call Meredith.

Meredith had a huge change thrust upon her when her husband announced that because of his work, they would need to move several hundred miles north. Meredith had thought she was settled for the rest of her life. She loved her city. She had lived there for 25 years. She knew all the right places to shop and eat. She also knew all the great museums, and the best routes to get to them—an accomplishment for someone who admits she has no sense of direction. Most of all, she loved the weather. The routinely sunny days made her feel sunny as well.

She had grown to love the home where she'd raised her 17-year-old son. She had fixed it up to suit her family's taste. Recently, she'd considered moving to another house—perhaps the Lord's way of preparing her for relocation—but she assumed it would be just a few miles away. Church and Bible study were close, and she'd made deep friendships in both places. Lifelong friends and some relatives also lived nearby. For 25 years she'd intentionally worked on building community. Leaving all of these connections was wrenching—like a firmly planted tree being pulled up by the roots.

Her husband felt bad for Meredith, but he had no choice about the move. He had to go where his company would be headquartered. Otherwise he would have to seek new employment and begin all over again. And there were very few other opportunities in his field where they now lived. Meredith understood this, but it didn't help her feelings of sadness and confusion. Just as with Mooch, change had been thrust upon her, and it wasn't of her doing.

Meredith struggled with her feelings. Why had God allowed this change to occur? How could He ask this of her? Would she be able to handle it? Her only consolation was in knowing that God loved her, and that "Jesus Christ is the same yesterday and today and forever" (Hebrews 13:8). Unlike Mooch, she had the unchangeable God to hold on to.

When it finally came time to leave, Meredith said a sad goodbye to me and her other friends, and we all cried. She tried to be brave, even taking photographs as she drove north to this new adventure. Her two cats rode in a carrier on the backseat of her car. As she and her husband pulled their vehicles into the driveway of their new home, a mostly Siamese cat streaked out from the backyard. Meredith felt God telling her He would bless her through this cat, though at that moment she couldn't understand how. She would later discover that Shadow was a stray, and he adopted her family, blessing them tremendously with his affectionate nature.

That first year after Meredith moved, we spent many hours on the phone together. I watched this brilliant, sensitive woman struggle through her adjustment while holding fast to God. She joined a Bible study similar to the one she had left. She and her husband found a church, and fellowshipping there helped to uphold her faith. But this wasn't her chosen city, she hadn't wanted to start over again, and she felt lonely—especially at first. It took six months before she was able to have deep conversations with two new friends.

Meredith has lived in her new city now for more than four years. God has used this change in her life in amazing ways. He has opened up a whole new career in speaking and writing that we know would not have happened had she remained where she was. Her faith has also gained new depth, as often happens when we cling to God through suffering. Meredith would still love to move back to her old city one day, and she wonders if that may happen sometime in the future, but she also knows that heaven will be her eternal home. Like the psalmist, she believes she will "see the goodness of the Lord in the land of the living," and that for now she needs to "be strong and take heart and wait for the Lord" (Psalm 27:13-14).

Mooch is content with his new home and family now. He bats his little toy mice all over the house. He loves our laps and leaps into them as often as he can, purring with delight when we pet him. He has adjusted to the change in his life, and we are so blessed to have him.

Meredith has adapted to her different life as well—due in part to the passing of time, but much more to the faithfulness of God. He has helped and encouraged her through her pain. Though everything else can change in a moment, God is the same, always and forever—and we can always count on Him.

I, the Lord, do not change (Malachi 3:6 NASB).

CONSIDER THIS

Have you ever had change thrust upon you? What was difficult and painful about it? How did you see God working? What positive things came out of it? Is there a change in your life right now that you need to surrender to the Lord?

Chasing Fears

Stand Firm in Your Faith

Courage is contagious. When a brave man takes a stand, the spines of others are stiffened.

Billy Graham

Evenings are a time when cats congregate in our backyard. Our own kitties are joined by several visiting neighbors. They curl up on the grass and porch, snoozing comfortably and feeling safe—till Stuart starts playing his favorite game. Stuart is our Welsh Corgi. He loves chasing cats. When we let him out, he dives at them, and they flee in terror, leaping over the back fence to safety—all except Milkshake.

Milkshake refuses to run in terror. He just stands his ground and watches the excitement. After Stuart clears the yard of the other felines, he and Milkshake sniff each other. They walk around in a circle and sometimes lie down together to rest. They seem to have reached an understanding. Stuart senses that Milkshake has faced his fears and refuses to be chased from his yard—and Stuart has succumbed to him.

Thinking of Milkshake's response to Stuart reminds me of a time when I had to stand my ground in my spiritual yard. In the early 1990s I went back to college to get my degree so I could become a teacher. I majored in philosophy and religious studies, and I had several interesting classes, some of which presented challenges to my Christian faith.

One professor taught that there were many ways to God. Her lectures and homework were prepared with this focus in mind. We were once assigned to write a mantra and say it several times a day. At first, I didn't see how I could do this. But I prayed about it, and God showed me how I could complete the homework, help myself, and honor my Savior. I could use Scripture as my mantra. I wrote down and memorized a portion of Proverbs 3 and the fruits of the Spirit from Galatians 5:22. Several times a day for the two-week period of this assignment, I stopped what I was doing and repeated these verses. I loved it!

Finally, it came time to share our mantra and what it had done for us with the other students in the class. When it was my turn, I began by thanking my teacher for the assignment. I told her my mantra had helped me immensely and I planned to keep saying it. Then I repeated those wonderful verses for the whole class to hear. Though she wasn't at all happy with the content of my assignment, I had done it, and she was forced to give me credit. My motive wasn't to anger my teacher. I'd simply sought to protect my spiritual yard and share my faith in an acceptable way.

This same professor didn't welcome dissension. If class members disagreed with her, she labeled them "not intellectual" and refused to accept their arguments. Many times I sensed her young students questioning her but not daring to speak up. I was much older, and I didn't feel intimidated by her—any more than Milkshake felt intimidated by Stuart. If I felt led to speak, I'd pray, ask my heavenly Father for the right words, and jump in. Several times other students came up to me after class and told me they'd been praying as I talked. I'd voiced what they'd wanted to, but they'd been too frightened to speak up. This professor was scaring them out of their spiritual yard, but she didn't scare me out of mine, and I made some new friends as a result.

One such friend was a young girl I sat and talked with a number of times after class, at her request. She told me she wanted to have the faith I did, but it seemed so hard. She said she had listened to how the professor believed, but she didn't really want that. What should she do?

I told her, "My way isn't hard or my way. It's Jesus' way. You don't have to do anything but accept His gift of salvation." She smiled and hugged me and asked me to pray for her. She felt confused and wasn't ready to take the step of asking Jesus into her heart, but she was gaining some courage to stand her ground and learn more about Him.

Just as Milkshake refused to be chased from his backyard, we can stand our ground in our yard of faith against those who would chase us out. We can study God's Word and know what it says. And as we pray for courage and strength, God will give us what we need. He loves us and wants us to be strong in our faith and encourage others to do the same so we can be strong in the world and witness for Him.

The Lord is my light and my salvation—whom shall I fear? The Lord is the stronghold of my life—of whom shall I be afraid? (Psalm 27:1).

CONSIDER THIS

Has anyone ever tried to scare you out of your yard of faith? What did they do or say? How did you respond? How might you stand your ground in the future, and encourage others to do so?

Kitten Love

Love One Another

When love and skill work together,
expect a masterpiece.

John Ruskin

When Tiger was a kitten, she was the cutest little gray tabby we'd ever seen. Not only was she adorable with irresistible blue eyes, but she also had an amazing personality. She made her human family feel as if she cared for each of us in a special way.

Tiger loved to snooze on the living room sofa. But no matter how deeply she was sleeping, if one of her humans entered, she would wake. She wouldn't just look up bleary eyed, the way many cats do. She would practically bounce off the sofa to rub against our legs. Then she'd plop down happily next to wherever we settled. Only if we left the room would she resume her sleep. Tiger cared more about her people than about finishing her nap.

At this time our family of five was bustling with activity. Our sons were teens and our daughter was seven. Each morning Tiger would make the rounds, going from bedroom to bedroom as if to say "good morning" to each member of her household. She'd repeat this every evening when we'd come home from our busy day. It seemed that she was on a mission to let her people know that each of us was important and precious to her.

Tiger would wander from room to room to say her hellos. If a door was closed, she'd meow sweetly to be let in. Once admitted, she'd sniff around, rub against any legs she could find, and respond happily to having her head petted. Then she'd continue her appointed work of checking in with each family member. After she'd made sure we were all home, she would pick a spot in one of our rooms to settle in for the night. She'd stay with each of us for about a week at a time and then move on to the next favored one.

Not only would Tiger make the rounds, but she'd also make us feel as if each of us was her exclusive favorite. We were quite amazed when we discovered this at dinner one night. Our daughter made a comment that she thought Tiger liked her best. Soon everybody else was staking the same claim. One of our sons knew he was tops with Tiger because each day when he curled up to read, she would climb onto his lap. I knew I was her favorite because she always kept me company when I folded laundry. Every one of us had a story about something Tiger did that convinced us we were special to her.

We have a "Tiger" in our church family too. Our founding pastor, Bill Wolitarsky, makes everyone feel special. He makes the rounds each Sunday before services start, checking up on each of us. It's not just a "Hi, how are you?" It's more like a "How are you doing…really?" Just the way he asks how your week was makes you know he truly cares and wants to know about your life. He's not one to whom you can say, "I'm fine, thank you" and expect to get away with it. He seems to have antennae. He can sense if you're really fine or not. One Sunday when I said "I'm okay" he responded with, "Was it a rough week?" He was right. It had been. I shared with him and he encouraged me. On another Sunday when things had been difficult, I knew if he sensed anything was wrong I'd burst into tears. So I tried to head off his probing. "I'm fine, Bill. How are you?" I asked. He responded by sharing his week with me, and I thought I had pulled it off. I hadn't. Next day, he phoned to express his concern. "You didn't seem quite right yesterday. What's going on?"

When I have something really exciting in my life, I know he'll want to hear all about it. When I've been in the midst of sorrow, he's called me to listen and say, "I just don't know how you are making it through! I'll pray for you."

Best of all, Bill celebrates the people in his life for who God has made us to be. He sees our potential as God's special children better than we see it ourselves. He's always been a loving shepherd who cares for and encourages each one of his flock.

When I began attending his church 20 years ago, I was a mom with three kids in tow. He celebrated my motherhood and encouraged me in that task. This was at a time in our culture when some people looked down on you if you told them you were just a homemaker. Not Bill. He said it was the most important job in the world.

I hadn't been at the church very long when I lost a relative in a car accident. Bill didn't know her and barely knew me, but he came to her memorial service. I was in deep grief that day, along with everyone else in my family. Then I noticed him standing there. I was astounded and felt supported in a way I'd never experienced before.

Over the last 20 years my husband has had eight angioplasties to clear blockages in arteries leading to his heart. Bill came to the hospital for every procedure, just to pray and give us encouragement. He didn't stay long, but knowing he cared enough to come for that few minutes of prayer gave us courage.

Bill doesn't do these things just for me. He's a shepherd to everyone. He makes the rounds just the way Tiger used to. Nor is he lofty or conceited about being a pastor. He is one of the most unassuming people I've ever known. One fellow church member told me he's like George Bailey in the movie *It's a Wonderful Life.*

He has no idea how many lives he has touched for the better. His humility is refreshing in our proud culture, and it enables him to love others selflessly. If one verse personifies him, it is Philippians 2:3: "Do nothing out of selfish ambition or vain conceit, but in humility consider others better than yourselves."

Jesus taught us how a shepherd should act; He is the Good Shepherd. But He doesn't want only pastors to be great caregivers. He said, "Love each other as I have loved you" (John 15:12). This command is for each of God's children. Bill is my role model in how to reach out and celebrate others, to show them someone cares about how they are feeling.

If a wonderful little kitten could make her entire family feel special as she made her daily rounds, just imagine how much more we can impact those we see every Sunday by taking a moment to ask about them, listen to them, and really care about them. It's a great way to obey our Lord's command to "love one another."

As we have opportunity, let us do good to all people, especially to those who belong to the family of believers (Galatians 6:10).

CONSIDER THIS

Are there people in your life whose care and concern has impacted you? How do they express it? How has it encouraged you? How might you make others feel cared about and special? Do you pray on your way to church that the Lord will use you this way in the family of God?

The Great Paper Towel Wars

Give Ground for God's Sake

The two powers which in my opinion constitute a wise man are those of bearing and forbearing.

Epictetus

I was seething. It was my house, my kitchen, my paper towels. How dare my cats unroll them all over the floor! It had gone on for days. I'd come down in the morning to a waterfall of white decorated with telltale claw marks. I'd even tried taping up the towel roll, but it didn't help that much. On this day, I'd had it with the feline towel takeover. Hey, just because my four cats lived mostly in my kitchen/den area didn't mean they could rule this part of my kingdom, right?

Alas, my kitties didn't share my viewpoint—but it was time to make them. I doubted my two older ones were to blame. That left Merlin and Muffin. In my anger and frustration, I wanted to make them fear the towels so they'd let them be. But just in time an inner voice cautioned, "You're going to ruin these cats!"

In that moment I realized the price of winning the towel war was too high. I did what I'd been resisting. I shoved the paper towels under my kitchen sink, where they lived for months. Instead of insisting on my own way, I chose to suffer some inconvenience and practice forbearance with my four-foots instead.

I've also had to make the same choice with two-footed housemates.

Because God has blessed me with a four-bedroom home and I live alone, now and then I open my door to friends in transition. I let them stay rent free till things sort out in their lives. I benefit too, because it gives me a break from a more solitary existence. And I figure since my temporary housemates don't pay, I still get to set the house rules.

Sometimes God figures otherwise.

One former housemate rattled my chain in the small daily details of life. She left lights on I wouldn't. She didn't always double lock the door. She put things back in slightly different places than I was accustomed to keeping them. This bugged the perfectionist in me. I kept correcting her till her own frustration bubbled over. She finally told me she felt as though she couldn't breathe—as though she couldn't do anything right. I realized I couldn't make her live exactly the way I did. I faced how stuck in my ways I'd become. I saw I could either ruin our friendship by demanding my rights or preserve it by giving ground. I backed off my perfectionism, and we're dear friends still.

With a more recent housemate, forbearance took the shape of her large computer monitor. She'd purchased a new flat screen monitor to replace it, but there was no space in her small, crowded room to store the old one comfortably. So she asked if she could leave it by my front door till she could dispose of it.

I wasn't thrilled about how that would look. I also knew how busy my friend was. I feared that monitor might sit by the door for weeks. I refused. Piled onto other pressures in her life, it was almost more than she could stand. She snapped that she'd find a way to deal with it, but her frustration was palpable. As I walked away, my conscience gnawed at me. It was my house; my call. And yet...even though I wasn't obligated to solve her problem, I knew God wanted me to practice a little forbearance. As I pondered the matter, I got an idea. I had an odd-shaped little closet where I stored mops, brooms, and cleaning supplies. There was space for the monitor, and it would be out of sight. At my suggestion, she stowed it there—and it remained for months. But that didn't matter. What did was that I had encouraged a friend. And besides, how can any small act of patience and tolerance on my part remotely compare to how forbearing God is?

Because I've given myself to Christ, I am God's child and His Spirit indwells me. But I still unravel paper towels of sin in my life. I'm still storing the big clunky monitor of my old nature, even though I have a new one. I don't keep my mind and heart spotlessly holy, as He would have them. And yet God is patient and tolerant with me. He shows me only what I can bear, and He refines me step by step.

My paper towels are back on their holder, and my cats now let them alone. The monitor's gone, and my housemate has a place of her own. Pets and people change, but God remains the same. With perfect forbearance, He keeps conforming us to the image of His Son so that we can bear with others as He bears with us.

Be completely humble and gentle; be patient, bearing with one another in love (Ephesians 4:2).

CONSIDER THIS

Who in your life do you find it most difficult to give ground to? What do they do that irritates you? Why does it? How do you respond? How might you alter that?

Community Cat

God's People Need Each Other

That is what our life in community is about. Each of us is like a little stone, but together we reveal the face of God to the world.

Henri Nouwen

There was never a cat like Pumpkin. If I had to describe him in one word, I would pick "personable." I think everyone who ever met him would agree. Phil and I have housed foreign students for 13 years, and most, if not all, have his photo. He has also been a favorite with several groups that have gathered in our home.

All our other cats have reacted quite differently when new people arrived. Most would flee in horror as the front door opened and stay hidden until the very last person left. Even those who were more sociable would come around briefly to investigate the strangers and then leave for other parts of the house. Pumpkin was completely different. He would give a special welcome to any newcomer, no matter who it was. He seemed to find peace in the midst of people.

We had the enormous privilege of watching Pumpkin be born. He was sociable even as a tiny kitten. In nearly every photo I have of the little feline family, Pumpkin is the kitten nearest to his mom. In my photos of the kittens alone, Pumpkin is always in the center of the group. He loved feline contact.

As he grew up, Pumpkin would follow the various members of our family around the house to settle with whichever person would accept his presence. He loved human contact too.

We had a Bible study in our home for three years, and week after week Pumpkin greeted each and every person warmly. After walking on nearly every available lap, Pumpkin chose one on which to curl up. It became a weekly joke as to who would be picked that night.

We also had a couples' group meet monthly in our home. After discussing marriage skills we would stand and hold hands to form a circle as we closed in prayer. Various people would pray as we stood there, and by the time we opened our eyes, Pumpkin would be sitting happily in the middle of the circle, eyes partly closed, looking as if he'd found the key to contentment. Perhaps he had.

Pumpkin's longing for contact and his ability to seek out people remind me of a verse in the Bible that says, "Let us not give up meeting together, as some are in the habit of doing, but let us encourage one another" (Hebrews 10:25).

Pumpkin got that verse right, but some people I know who call themselves Christians don't make meeting together a regular part of their lives. They may seek community occasionally, but they don't make it their habit.

I know two people in this category. We'll call one Ben and the other Julia. Ben stopped attending church regularly while in college because he said he got nothing out of it. People tried to explain to Ben that God had established the Sabbath as a holy day, a day of rest and sacred assembly (Leviticus 23:3). They told Ben the assembly was a gathering of believers, but their arguments fell on deaf ears, and he gradually stopped going to church altogether. In his mind community didn't matter.

Julia stopped going to church for a completely different reason. She said there were too many hypocrites there. Perhaps that was merely an excuse because she was living with her boyfriend and didn't want to deal with any awkward questions that might be asked.

It's not easy to live for Jesus in our culture because so much of it opposes what pleases God. Part of coming together in community is to help us who believe. Both Ben and Julia still consider themselves Christians, but neither has fervency for Jesus. Billy Graham said, "Churchgoers are like coals in a fire. When they cling together, they keep the flame aglow; when they separate, they die out." That's what happened with Ben and Julia. They should have taken a lesson from Pumpkin and sought community. When we go to be with God's children week after week, our passion for the Lord is fanned and our faith is strengthened. What's more, just being together makes the promise of Jesus come alive: "Where two or three come together in my name, there am I with them" (Matthew 18:20). He is a Savior who loves gatherings of His people.

I have a friend who has gone to church twice and often three times a week for more than 50 years. She says she's known times of great discouragement as well as great excitement, but she went regardless of how she felt because it was the thing to do. She has never regretted being in community. Her faith is one I long to emulate. That's why I push to be involved, even when it's tough. And just as Pumpkin found his contentment in community, so I find encouragement and strength in the midst of my brothers and sisters in Christ as we worship our great God together.

You are no longer foreigners and aliens, but fellow citizens with God's people and members of God's household, built on the foundation of the apostles and prophets, with Christ Jesus himself as the chief cornerstone (Ephesians 2:19-20).

CONSIDER THIS

Have you ever tried to be a Lone Ranger Christian? How did it affect your life and your walk with the Lord? How have you been blessed by being in close community with other believers? How might you bless others?

Legacy Lost

Pass On Your Faith

Train a child in the way he should go, and when he is old he will not turn from it.

PROVERBS 22:6

Kitty always taught her kittens to love their human masters. She let them come up to us so they could learn to know us. We played with them and took care of them. But it was different with her last litter. We had just moved to a new home and Kitty wasn't comfortable there, so she was a little too nervous and busy to do this.

We gave that last litter tire names because Kitty kept them in a stack of old tires. One of them, Michelin, recently had kittens of her own. She has been training her babies well. She has shown them where the food is, where they can sleep, where they can play safely in our yard and a host of other good cat living rules. But she has also taught them one sad thing: to be afraid of us, their people. When they see us coming, these little ones will run and hide. If we happen to get close to them, they hiss at us like wildcats. Michelin's mother never taught her to know us, so this wasn't something she understood, and she didn't pass this legacy on to her babies, either.

Knowing God is also a legacy that may fade if it isn't passed on. We have some precious friends, a young family with small children who live in our community. The parents are bright, hardworking, wonderful people who know Jesus as their personal Savior. They had gone to church since birth and understood the importance of worshipping God with others and fellowshipping with believers. When they had their own children, they took them to church and Sunday school too.

But, like Kitty, they became distracted when their lives became busier. Soccer games and bicycle trips and camping began to take up their time. Church became less important to them. They still took their children to a Wednesday night program which focused on Scripture memorization, but they no longer worshipped and fellowshipped on Sundays.

Because they had once attended church, the children felt this change. Their daughter even told me she missed the kids' choir and other activities. But over time, this lapsed legacy began to take its toll. The youngsters' attitudes began to change. Their behavior suffered. I sensed a feeling of self-centeredness and indifference toward their heavenly Master.

The young parents saw this. They realized they were cheating themselves and their dear children out of the precious gift of a Christ-centered family. They came back to church and began to pray together as a family. Now they are growing strong in their faith, enjoying one another, and serving God in all parts of their lives.

God desires that His people pass on the legacy of faith in Him to future generations. One way this was done in Old Testament times was through festivals. God commanded these observances to remind the people of what He had done and teach successive generations to love and trust their Master. After Moses mandated the celebration of the first Passover, he told the people, "Obey these instructions as a lasting ordinance for you and your descendants. When you enter the land that the Lord will give you as he promised, observe this ceremony. And when your children ask you, 'What does this ceremony mean to you?' then tell them, 'It is the Passover sacrifice to the Lord, who passed over the houses of the Israelites in Egypt and spared our homes when he struck down the Egyptians' " (Exodus 12:24-27).

Michelin and her kittens lost out on the joy of knowing their masters. Not so our friends and their children. They are growing strong in the love and knowledge of God. And because this rich legacy of faith was nurtured instead of lost, these youngsters will have it to pass on to their children and the generations to come.

These are the commands, decrees and laws the LORD your God directed me to teach you to observe in the land that you are crossing the Jordan to possess, so that you, your children and their children after them may fear the LORD your God as long as you live by keeping all his decrees and commands that I give you, and so that you may enjoy long life (Deuteronomy 6:1-2).

CONSIDER THIS

Are you passing on a legacy of faith to the children and grandchildren in your family? If so, what are some ways you do this? If not, how might you encourage them to know and love the Lord?

All in the Family

Make God's House Welcoming

Do not forget to entertain strangers,
for by so doing some people have enter-
tained angels without knowing it.

HEBREWS 13:2

Sweetie was a lost little kitten who found us. She wandered into our backyard one day and curled up on the porch on one of our cat pillows. Our own kitties sat tightly intertwined, as if to protect themselves from the tiny trespasser. Because they were so unfriendly, Sweetie got the pillow all to herself. She had plenty of room and she was probably comfortable—yet she seemed so alone. We checked around, but nobody knew whom she belonged to. We could see that she wanted to belong to us, so we let her stay. But our cats were not so sure.

Night after night I would go out to see how Sweetie was doing. For a while it was always the same. Our kitties huddled together for warmth. Sweetie lay by herself. I wondered what she had to do to prove herself and join the group.

Still, she never gave up. During the day she stayed near the others, watching them. When night came, she slept by herself. She didn't push herself on them, she just ate and slept close by. Slowly, they began accepting her. Now she lives with them and is part of their tight-knit little group. It is good to see her being included rather than ignored.

Watching Sweetie try to join our cat family made me think, "How does my church family treat newcomers who come and want to belong?" There was a time many years ago when I went to a church that treated visitors as if they were strangers in our yard. Like Sweetie, they were not welcomed as they should have been. I'm sure the looks they got from many in our congregation convinced them not to come back.

An old friend described walking into a church like that in his younger years. He felt as though he'd walked into someone else's home by mistake. He left never wanting to go to church again. But after he married, his wife convinced him to try it one more time. They visited the congregation I'm now attending and were greeted warmly. Many people welcomed them. They didn't have to prove themselves in any way. Just by being there, they were accepted. My friend said this is what he thought a church should be like. He felt as though he were coming home.

Our church is growing wonderfully, welcoming new people from all over who feel accepted as part of God's family. But unintentional oversights still happen. Just recently, I watched from the choir loft as a visitor was seated in an empty pew. I could see the lonely look on her face as she sat all by herself. But the situation was soon corrected. When the service was over, she was greeted by several people. She started smiling, feeling the love and warmth around her. She was welcomed with Christ's love by the family of God.

My friend and coauthor Marion Wells tells a similar story about the Bible study class she has long been attending. The class is a mix of people from many different churches. Their leadership thought the atmosphere was welcoming, but they were mistaken. One day a class member told them newcomers often felt lost and alone. She said even she didn't always feel that welcomed when she walked in the door. The leadership took the critique to heart. Now greeters welcome people at the door each week. Old-timers get a hug and a personal word. Visitors are introduced to others and made to feel at home. Everyone is treated like family and given personal attention, and this has helped the class grow.

Cats are territorial, so it's not surprising that it took time for Sweetie to be welcomed into the family group. But God wants His people to reach out, not pull back. Why not open your heart, welcome strangers as friends, and watch how God will bless.

For two whole years Paul stayed there in his own rented house and welcomed all who came to see him (Acts 28:30).

CONSIDER THIS

Is your church welcoming or standoffish toward strangers? Why do you think that is? How do people respond if the newcomers seem different somehow? How might your church and you personally make visitors feel more at home?

Part V

Who's Top Cat?

God Reigns over Us for Our Good

RACKY

The Miracle of Birth

God Is in the Details

I believe in Christianity as I believe that the sun has risen: not only because I see it, but because by it I see everything else.

C.S. Lewis

We sat around in awe that morning. Racky, our adorable calico cat, was giving birth and we had the privilege of watching. My husband, two teenaged sons, and our six-year-old daughter were gathered around the big box we had readied just for this occasion.

It had all begun at 3 a.m., when Racky was sleeping close to me in my bed. She had her body tight against mine, and my hand was resting on her pregnant belly, when suddenly she let out a low growling noise. I awoke, touched her tummy, which was as hard as a rock, and realized labor had begun. I roused my husband, and we carefully moved her into her big box. Then we awakened our children.

We watched in wonder as Racky yowled, pressed hard, and a kitten popped out. It actually didn't look like a kitten at all. It looked more like a rat in a sack. Once the kitten was birthed, Racky focused on getting the sack off. She worked hard, licking and absorbing the sack so the kitten could breathe and be free. It was a curious sight to see our little cat laboring so furiously over each tiny new life. She was tired when the fourth and last kitten was born, and we had to encourage her to clean that one up. But she did, and then she lay back, completely out of strength. We relaxed as we saw each new kitten on a teat, getting vital nourishment from her. And she finally looked peaceful, although very tired.

We had witnessed a true miracle, one that God invented…birth! What an awesome plan! Equally and perhaps even more amazing is when God births a spiritual baby.

The Gospel of John tells about a highly respected religious leader named Nicodemus who had seen and heard Jesus firsthand. He wanted to talk with Jesus, recognizing something great in Him. Perhaps Nicodemus was curious and wanted to know more. Perhaps he had a hunger to be closer to God. We're not sure of his motives, but we do know that because of his peers' animosity toward Jesus, Nicodemus went to see Him in the dark of night. Nicodemus didn't want them to know he was considering Jesus' claims. When he found Jesus, Nicodemus said, "Rabbi, we know you are a teacher who has come from God. For no one could perform the miraculous signs you are doing if God were not with him" (John 3:2). Jesus surprised him by getting straight to what He knew Nicodemus needed, telling him that "no one can see the kingdom of God unless he is born again" (John 3:3). That confused Nicodemus, who, relating only to physical birth, spoke about the impossibility of getting into a womb again. Jesus then clarified that He was talking about spiritual birth: "Flesh gives birth to flesh, but the Spirit gives birth to spirit" (John 3:6).

The Holy Spirit, the third Person of the triune Godhead, is the One who gives birth to God's children. Only then can we be aware of the kingdom of God, which is now invisible but nonetheless completely real. Being born from above is a mysterious event that takes more faith than knowledge. That's why little children can become Christians, even though they don't know much. Recently my husband and I were treated to a marvelous message on our answering machine. Our little grandson Owen said, "Hi, Grandma and Grandpa. I just asked Jesus into my heart. I'm excited! Bye." We were delighted that he wanted to tell us. When I spoke with his mom, she said Owen had been talking about Jesus to her, and said, "Mom, Jesus is bigger than the earth! He's huge." Owen doesn't understand the Word of God becoming flesh, Emmanuel (God with us), or that Jesus is the propitiation for our sins, but he does know Jesus died for us and is alive today. And Owen knows Jesus loves him and is his Friend. From the human angle we receive the Lord Jesus: "If you confess with your mouth, 'Jesus is Lord,' and believe in your heart that God raised him from the dead, you will be saved" (Romans 10:9). Yet, from the heavenly angle, God brings about a new creation: "Therefore, if anyone is in Christ, he is a new creation; the old has gone, the new has come!" (2 Corinthians 5:17). Just as the kittens were new creations physically, so each person who receives Jesus is made spiritually new.

I didn't come to Jesus as a child; I was an adult, but I didn't know much more than Owen did. After I asked Jesus in, though, I saw signs that I was changed. Prior to my new birth, I had wanted to love people without reservation, but I felt I had to protect myself from possible harm and that made me hold back. When I became a new creation in Christ, however, I felt a fresh, new, unconditional love for others. Now I understand that what I experienced is a fruit of the Holy Spirit.

Some people, when they are born again, lose their fear of death. Other people see colors more vividly and are thrilled with God's creation, as if viewing it for the first time. Still others have a new sense of belonging because they suddenly realize they are in God's family. There are various experiences that may accompany the new birth. And for some individuals there may not be an experience per se, but an understanding that they have been saved from their sins.

After their birth the kittens needed nourishment for health and growth. Spiritual babes need nourishment for these reasons too. I was blessed to be in a strong, in-depth Bible study group which gave me many hours of learning from the pure spiritual milk of God's Word.

Beyond the birthing, the Holy Spirit begins to work in our lives to rid us of all the bad stuff we call baggage. Just as Racky licked the sack off each kitten to free it, so the Holy Spirit cleans us up so we can be free. For the kittens it took just a moment. For God's children, it may take a lifetime.

It took a while for my friend Lilly. She had a very rough childhood—abuse, loneliness, instability. You name it and she probably experienced it. This created destructive patterns that became habits that bound her. When she met Jesus she was filled with hope, and the Holy Spirit began His work on this new creation. Unlike the kittens, she realized she had decisions to make about whether to walk in the new life or go back to the old ways. It was a battle that took years, but as she chose over and over to walk in the new path, the old became only a memory. Now she is a vibrant woman teaching kids about Jesus and helping other women to walk in freedom because she has allowed God to clean her up.

As I mentioned earlier, the kittens didn't look like kittens when they were first born. We don't look like Jesus right away, either, but that's where we're headed. In Romans 8:29, the apostle Paul explains that God is conforming each of His children to the image of His Son. If we cooperate in that process, we will look more and more like Jesus as we move along on this journey we call life.

What a wonderful God we have. We can do nothing to earn His favor. Rather, it is He who does it all to a willing heart: birth, freedom, and ministry. Our spiritual birth gives us eternal life, which begins the moment we are born again and doesn't stop, even at death. He who birthed us waits to receive us, perfected at last, to be with Him forever.

As many as received Him, to them He gave the right to become children of God, even to those who believe in His name, who were born, not of blood nor of the will of the flesh nor of the will of man, but of God (John 1:12-13 NASB).

CONSIDER THIS

Have you asked Jesus into your heart? Did any new experiences follow your new birth? What changes have you seen in your life since? What remnants of the sack of your old self is God's Spirit still freeing you from? How can you cooperate with Him?

Sign Language for Cats and People

Look for God's Leading

God's will is not an itinerary, but an attitude.

Andrew Dhuse

Some things just seem to go together: peanut butter and jelly, ham and eggs, and cats and counters. My cats used my kitchen counters as both parking lot and freeway. I wasn't always around to stop them, and at one point there were four of them against one of me. So I let things slide a bit—till a housemate objected. She graciously pointed out that the feet that traversed the surfaces where food was prepared had also been digging in a litter box. And they hadn't had a foot bath in between.

Realizing she had a point and not wanting to offend her sensibilities, I agreed to work harder to discourage my four-foots' counter-walking. To do so we kept a small squirt bottle handy. When Merlin, Muffin, Barney, or Misty ventured onto a surface where they didn't belong, we sprayed them with water. That is, we did at first. Pretty soon, it wasn't necessary. All we had to do was show them the bottle and they fairly flew off the forbidden counter. That bottle became a form of "kitty sign language." It said, "You're where you don't belong, and if you don't move, and fast, you are going to be hosed in the mush."

Sign language doesn't only work with cats. It can work with babies too. It worked with me—or so my mother says. I'd started to teethe, and when my mouth hurt, I cried. Mom mashed baby aspirin into applesauce to ease my pain. I came to connect that action with relief. As soon as I saw it, I stopped bawling. Mom noticed and started to make the applesauce mixing motion at my first sobs. I knew help was coming and hushed till her remedy was ready. I'd learned to understand Mom's "sign language."

God also uses "sign language" to communicate with His children. In Old Testament times, His signs were often visual and dramatic. The rainbow was a sign of God's promise never again to destroy the earth by water. The ten plagues were signs to Pharaoh and his people that the Israelites' God was greater than theirs and He wanted the Egyptians to let His people go. The Lord also led the Israelites through the desert in a pillar of cloud and a pillar of fire—visible signs of His presence.

Now God's children have His Spirit living within us, and His sign language is often more subtle. God may use gentle nudges or impressions to indicate His will. Years ago when my dad had cancer, I got such a nudge out of nowhere to drive the hour and a half to my parents' home and spend some time with them. I obeyed on the spot. The day after I left them to return to my own home, my father took his life. God knew what was about to happen and prodded me to go and see him, knowing it would be my last chance.

God also uses His Word to guide us. I don't believe in so-called "holy hopscotch"—hunting and pecking through the Bible and randomly pulling a verse out of context to justify claiming a particular thing is God's will. But I do think that in addition to the primary meaning of Scripture, God's Spirit can take a particular passage and apply it in a more specific way to our lives right now. I was a relatively new believer when I graduated from college. An uncle of mine invited me to work for his health charity in Los Angeles. I spent a few days there to check it out, but the situation felt rather scary. I'd also applied to join a training program with a Christian ministry. My parents weren't thrilled about that option, but they didn't forbid it. As for me, I was trying to seek God's will. And then, as I was reading my Bible, I came upon James 4:13-15: "Now listen, you who say, 'Today or tomorrow we will go to this or that city, spend a year there, carry on business and make money.' Why, you do not even know what will happen tomorrow. What is your life? You are a mist that appears for a little while and then vanishes. Instead, you ought to say, 'If it is the Lord's will, we will live and do this or that.' "

That verse, combined with my acceptance to the training program and my own heart's desires, led me to choose the ministry option. I was there two years. It was a time of tremendous growth and grounding. Following that period, I wound up working for my uncle after all, but I was much better equipped to deal with the situation because I had grown in my faith and Bible knowledge.

God also has other nonverbal signs He uses to indicate His will, like having peace or a lack of it about a course of action. I've learned to distinguish this kind of leading from the more iffy signs or fleeces we sometimes ask Him for. God's ways of guiding us are consistent, and we can learn to recognize them, as my cats did the squirt bottle and I did Mom's applesauce mixing motion.

How marvelous that the King of the universe cares about the details of my life. How marvelous that He seeks to direct my steps. I am eager to watch for and follow His leading because I am convinced that His sign language is a sign of His love.

I will instruct you and teach you in the way you should go; I will counsel you and watch over you (Psalm 32:8).

CONSIDER THIS

What are some means God has used to confirm His leading in your life? Did you recognize them at the time? How did you respond, and what happened? Has the way you seek His leading changed as you've matured in your faith? If so, how?

Huffy Muffy

Give Space, As God Does

Patience is the ability to count down before you blast off.

Author Uknown

My cat Muffin is a sensitive soul. She needs a gentle touch. This day I blew it with her—big time! I'd put all three cats in an upstairs guest bathroom so workmen could finish a little remodeling project in my kitties' normal downstairs haunts. But I didn't want them pawing through the linen closet, where I'd stored some Christmas decorations. The closet's folding door was balky, and it wouldn't stay shut by itself. I'd propped it closed. When I checked back later, the door was ajar and Muffy was curled up inside.

I was peeved. I was also a bit too worried about my Christmas stuff. In my pique, I was overly rough with the door and my cat as I pulled her out. She became totally spooked. She cringed and snarled. My heart sank. This sweet, affectionate ball of fur who normally purred at my touch clearly wanted no part of me.

I carried Muffin into my office. I tried to cuddle her, but she ran away the instant I released her. I knew deep inside I should let her cool off, but I felt desperate for her forgiveness. As she scooted into corners and under my desk, I kept pursuing her. I scooped her up again and again, trying to get her to purr. She hissed and snarled and stiffened instead. Finally I carried her into my own bathroom's shower stall. I closed the glass door, set her down, and plopped beside her. I hoped if she was loose, but in an enclosed space with me, I could coax her to warm up.

Wrong move! Muffin crouched and sprang for a ledge high up on the shower wall. She missed and fell back to the floor with a thud. I was stunned. I hadn't realized just how frantic she was to escape me. I saw that she could be badly hurt if I pushed things any further. I put her back in my office, closed the door, and left her alone.

I don't remember all I did for the next few hours. I do recall that I swam in my pool and prayed. I think I ate dinner. Even when I went back into the same room with Muffin, I didn't force the issue. By day's end she'd returned to her old purr-ball self. She did have one further flashback of fear a few days later, but she got over that too, when I gave her space to do so. I just had to be patient and realize I couldn't force her feelings.

God knows we may need time to deal with our feelings toward Him as well. He knows that the troubles of this world sometimes make us feel angry and let down and even abandoned by Him. While He is never deserving of this, He understands our human frailty. He's patient with us. He gives us space—more space than we're sometimes inclined to give each other.

Recently, I was tempted to press a friend who was struggling with her feelings toward God. She'd just had one more in a series of painful disappointments. She'd been praying for God to rescue her and wondered if He would come through. I felt that God might be offering help…but she might be missing it because it wasn't in the form she'd been hoping for.

I wrote her an e-mail. I quoted a popular story about a man whose house was being engulfed by flood waters. As the waters rose higher, first a boat and then a helicopter came to rescue him. He turned them down, explaining he'd prayed and God would save him. Eventually he drowned. He entered heaven. He came before the throne of God and asked the Lord why He hadn't saved him, as he'd fervently begged. And God said He'd tried. He'd sent a boat. He'd sent a helicopter...

I started to send the e-mail. God said, "Stop!"

I parked the e-mail in "send later." When it was later, I deleted it altogether. I sensed God's Spirit telling me it wasn't time. My friend was in too much pain. She wasn't ready to hear this. God was giving her space to deal with her feelings...and I must do the same.

Some days later I was speaking with her husband. He mentioned telling her a story—the exact same story in my e-mail. He'd told it in the context of making a decision that might help turn things around for her. At that later point she'd been ready to hear it, and it had actually encouraged positive forward motion.

God knows His kids. He understands that feelings can't be forced. He doesn't crowd us to get His own needs met, as I did with Muffin. He gives us space. His timing is perfect. He acts for our good and not His own because He loves us.

If we're led by God's Spirit, we can love that way too, and be patient with others as He is with us.

As God's chosen people, holy and dearly loved, clothe yourselves with compassion, kindness, humility, gentleness and patience (Colossians 3:12).

CONSIDER THIS

Have you ever become impatient with people and pressured them inappropriately? What did you do? What was the result? How might you be more patient in the future?

Cat-astrophic Salad

God Is Bigger than Our Bloopers

I have lived, Sir, a long time, and the longer I live, the more convincing proofs I see of this truth—that God governs in the affairs of men.

Benjamin Franklin

Today was the day. I'd been planning to participate in the church cook-off for months, and here it was. Everyone's entries would be sampled and judged, and small trophies would be given to the winners. Usually I don't cook from a book, but this time I had gone through many, looking for a unique recipe. I'd finally found it—a special salmon salad with fruit.

Kitty was living in the house at that time, and she must have loved the aroma from the salmon, as any cat would. She was all over me. I gave her a little piece of fish and then made her go outside. This was a gift for our church friends, not for her—or so I thought.

The finished product was beautiful. It had salmon, cantaloupe, and other things in a special dressing. Grapes of different varieties added incredible color and life to this appetizing dish. I put it in a lovely china bowl and covered it carefully.

My nephew Mark was with me that day. I asked him to carry the dish to the car and guard it with his life while I grabbed a few other necessities. Then I would drive us both to the church. Just as I was about to go outside, Mark came back. He approached me warily. "Connie, I put the salad on top of the car for just a second and Kitty jumped up and knocked it off onto the dirt."

"Oh, Mark, come on, there's no time for kidding here. We have to go to church," I told him.

He said, "I'm not kidding." And he handed me the empty bowl.

I couldn't believe what had happened to my masterpiece. But I was determined not to let a cat-induced catastrophe ruin things. We rushed outside and scooped up whatever parts of the salad hadn't touched the dirt or been licked by my cat. We put what we'd salvaged in half a cantaloupe shell, added a little greenery, and it actually looked pretty good.

We had a great time at the church dinner. Nobody knew what had happened to the salad. And it won first prize!

In retrospect, what I did might not have been the best idea. My human ingenuity isn't flawless. But God's thoughts and ways are perfect, and He has all power. He can use even my mistakes to accomplish His purposes—as He did in an airport on a certain night long ago.

I was 18 years old. I had gone to Japan with 40 other young people to work with our missionaries and see the country. It was a wonderful learning time. I'd made new friends from all over Japan, the United States, and Canada. I'd shared the gospel with many people. I'd taught little Japanese children to sing "Jesus Loves Me."

When we got on the plane to leave, I was sad to go, but I was also ready to head home. I had 85 cents in my wallet and a heart and mind full of memories. We had a layover in Honolulu. Our chaperones wanted some time to themselves. They asked if we minded being on our own. I felt a bit concerned, but my companions said they'd take care of me.

Because I had less than a dollar and no credit cards, I couldn't do much. One of the guys in our group gave me 20 dollars. The others decided where they'd go for the night and asked me to come with them. But I wanted to spend my money on Hawaiian food and gifts, not a hotel. So I told them I'd stay in the airport for the night, and they left me there.

I knew this was an unwise decision. We'd been instructed throughout the trip never to go off alone. Now here I was, all by myself in a huge airport for the night. I knew it was disobedient to our leaders and to God—but I had made up my mind.

I put my luggage in a locker and began walking and window-shopping. It was only 7 p.m., so I had lots of time. After visiting every shop at least twice, I bought a little food and sat down to eat. After just a few minutes, a young man in a military uniform sat down beside me.

We began to chat. He was from the Midwest and was the youngest in his family. He was on his way to Vietnam. I think we sensed each other's fear, but talking brought us peace. We shared our lives for hours and hours. As the sun began to rise, we stood by the window and watched it together. I asked if I could pray for him. He was grateful. So we spent some wonderful time talking to the Lord. When it was time for him to go, he thanked me and hugged me. His whole countenance had changed from fear to peace. He left with a smile and a confident stride, knowing God was with him.

My original decision to stay in the airport alone was wrong, but God used it for His purposes. He did the same with a biblical character named Samson. God meant for Samson to help deliver Israel from the Philistines. But though he had enormous strength, Samson lacked discipline and wisdom. His missteps culminated in a horrible mistake. He told a Philistine woman named Delilah the source of his strength. " 'No razor has ever been used on my head,' he said, 'because I have been a Nazirite set apart to God since birth. If my head were shaved, my strength would leave me, and I would become as weak as any other man' " (Judges 16:17).

Once Samson's secret was revealed, his enemies shaved off his hair, put out his eyes, and threw him in prison. But as time passed, his hair began to grow back. Then one day the Philistines had a celebration in the temple of their god. They dragged Samson out to entertain them. And Samson begged God to give him strength just one more time. He shoved on the pillars supporting the temple and brought the building down on his enemies, slaying more in his death than in his life. Despite his missteps, God's purposes had been served.

I never saw that young soldier again, but I know our time together helped him, and it is a favorite memory of that trip. I am grateful that God is bigger than my mistakes. It comforts me to know that when I, in my humanness, knock the gorgeous salmon salad of His perfect will to the dirt, He can scoop up the pieces, rearrange them, and use them for His glory.

We know that in all things God works for the good of those who love him, who have been called according to his purpose (Romans 8:28).

CONSIDER THIS

Have you ever made a mistake that God salvaged and used for His purposes? What happened? What did you learn? How is this a comfort to you in your life now?

Who Owns Whom?

God's Agenda Is Best

Young man, young man, your arm's
too short to box with God.

James Weldon Johnson

I could feel the steam coming off my head. For what seemed like the umpteenth time, I had found a "pile" on the kitchen floor instead of in the cat box. The evidence pointed to Muffin as the guilty party. I'd expressed my displeasure and tried to deter her, but so far all my efforts had failed, and my frustration was mounting.

I'd heard that cats do this kind of thing when they get their dander up. I'd dumped a rug Muffin liked that had grown pungent. Maybe she was miffed about that. Or she might have been trying to tell me I needed to spend more time with her—and she was right. Still, I wasn't about to put up with her feline temper tantrum. I hated the concept of being controlled by my cat. After all, who owned whom? I carried her to the scene of her crime and held her nose to the evidence. "You're a nine-pound cat, and you don't run this house," I growled.

At which point, God whispered to my heart, "Marion, you're the nine-pound cat!"

In that instant, the spiritual tables turned. I realized I was just like my cat. I'd been throwing a temper tantrum too. I'd wanted the Lord to meet my needs my way. I'd tried to pray Him onto my agenda. I'd wanted Him to boost my self-esteem by giving me career success. I'd hoped a novel I wrote would become a bestseller. When it languished instead, I grew angry with God and left Him "piles" of bitterness and rebellion.

Deep inside, I knew what God desired. He wanted me to base my self-worth on Him and the value He placed on me. He wanted me to focus on heavenly results, not earthly ones. He wanted to grow my obedience and discipline my pride. But instead of submitting, I wrestled...and wrestled...and wrestled. I searched the dot-coms for my book's sales ranking, as if willing God to boost it. Instead of writing, I frittered away my time. I writhed in my self-inflicted pain, wondering if my career was ending and my dreams would die. And all the while, God waited.

A friend once painted a poignant picture of what it's like to wrestle with God. She described it as trying to climb up on God's throne. We struggle and struggle, but we can't manage the feat. And so at last we fall back and surrender. And our gracious loving Father reaches down and lifts us onto His lap.

When I gave up at last, God lifted me. He gave me an agent through that less than blockbuster novel. He led me to do a whole different kind of book, a devotional for dog lovers. Two friends and I teamed up on the project. My agent found us a publisher, and *Four Paws from Heaven* was born. We have heard that our book is encouraging others and touching hearts with God's love. God is using all this to change my heart too. I'm pleased that our book is doing well, but its ministry matters even more. And God has grown that ministry to include a devotional for cat lovers, of which this story is a part. He met my needs His way, not mine, and as always, His way proved best.

Muffin the cat has only a limited understanding of what she's doing. She just knows when she's unhappy or I'm displeased. I comprehend far more. I know deep down that I can't run my world any better than she can run hers. I know God wants me to submit to Him, seek His agenda in prayer, and do what He tells me, even if it's not what I had in mind.

God sees not just our immediate need, but the eternal picture. He always knows what's best. So trust in Him, offer praise, and watch what He will do.

Then Job replied to the Lord: "I know that you can do all things; no plan of yours can be thwarted...My ears had heard of you but now my eyes have seen you. Therefore I despise myself and repent in dust and ashes" (Job 42:1-2,5-6).

CONSIDER THIS

Have you ever wrestled with God and then discovered His way was best? What happened? How has it affected your faith? Where might you offer Him praise in your life right now?

New Cat on the Block

God Puts People Together for His Purposes

Everything that irritates us about others can lead us to an understanding of ourselves.

Carl Jung

My two older cats, Misty and Barney, were ten and eleven when I got Muffin. In time I decided she needed a younger playmate. My first attempt to provide one failed when the kitten died after just a few short weeks. But I was determined to try again. That's when I found Merlin.

Merlin was a big, friendly, male orange tabby a rescue group had put up for adoption. He loved people and got along great with most other four-foots. At roughly ten months, he was just a bit younger than Muffin. I thought he was perfect.

Muffin thought otherwise.

It's not normally in the nature of cats to welcome newcomers with open paws, but Muffin threw the biggest hissy fit of all my felines. Her fur was bristling. Her dander was up. She'd eye Merlin from a few feet away, snarling in fear and outrage at this new cat on the block. I'm sure I told her, on at least one occasion, "Hey, I got him for you." Even if she'd understood me, I doubt that would have impressed her. She'd likely have hissed, "He's not what I wanted at all. I'd much rather have played with a catnip mouse, and you wouldn't have had to feed it!"

Muffin and Merlin eventually reached an uneasy détente, but they never became best pals. Merlin played a bit too rough for my Ragdoll princess. When he pounced on her, she screeched as if she were being killed. Imperfect human that I am, I'm not sure I picked the best cat to put into Muffin's life.

God, on the other hand, is perfect, and He picks just the right people to put into mine, even though I sometimes hiss in the beginning too—the way I did with Joy.

I was ten when Joy came to work for our family. I didn't know God then or realize His hand was in it. I just knew she didn't meet my childish expectations. Our former housekeeper had been young and pretty. Joy was old enough to have a grown daughter, and her features weren't especially attractive. She was wrinkled and arthritic too. Snotty kid that I was, I judged her by her outward appearance and rejected her.

Joy saw my reaction. She could have responded in hurt or anger, but she knew Jesus as her personal Savior and Lord. She had an inner beauty I had yet to discover, and she had God's perspective. She laughed off my response and resolved to win me over.

In short order, she did. Her humor, her winsomeness, and most of all her love, captured me. I was my parents' only child. I was also neurotic…though not for that reason. Joy talked me through my growing pains, becoming like a second mom. When my parents took occasional vacations, they left me in her care. But God knew she had a larger role to play than just surrogate parent, counselor, and friend. He placed her in my life to be a constant, consistent, powerful witness for Him.

My Jewish family didn't believe that Jesus was the prophesied Messiah, the Word made flesh, the Lamb of God who died to atone for our sins. Joy never tried to push her faith on us. She just lived it in front of us, day after day. She read her Bible. She talked about the Holy Spirit's guidance. We knew her arthritis kept her in pain a good deal of the time, but she wouldn't give in. If her health was shaky, her walk with the Lord was robust and strong. It gave her strength—even when it came to dealing with me. Difficult as I could be at times, she kept right on loving and forgiving me, and she never gave up.

When I was 14, my family moved from New York to California. Joy came also, staying with us two more years. It was there, in my parents' kitchen, that we had a conversation I never forgot. I'd been spiritually searching. I asked Joy if I had to believe in Jesus to get to heaven. She didn't duck the question. Gently, lovingly, she told me that I did.

Not long afterward, Joy was called back to her home state of West Virginia to help care for a dying loved one. She remained there. I went off to college. At 19, I asked Jesus to forgive my sins and come into my heart. I came to believe that He is the One of whom the prophet Isaiah wrote, "Surely he took up our infirmities and carried our sorrows, yet we considered him stricken by God, smitten by him, and afflicted. But he was pierced for our transgressions, he was crushed for our iniquities; the punishment that brought us peace was upon him, and by his wounds we are healed" (Isaiah 53:4-5). As I grew in my faith, I began to realize how God had used Joy in my life to nurture me and plant His seeds of truth.

More years passed. When I was in my mid-twenties, a business trip took me to West Virginia. My parents had kept in touch with Joy, and I knew her health had worsened. I drove a rental car to the small town where she lived and spent a few last precious hours with her. We rejoiced together in the faith I'd found, and she introduced me to her family. Not long afterward, she died.

When I first met Joy I never dreamed what role God destined her to play in my life. That's been true of others too. Some of those I drew back from when I first met them grew into my closest friends, but other relationships remained bumpy, like Muffin's and Merlin's. No matter. God has used them all.

God puts people into our lives for a purpose—to grow and mold and refine us. He mixes us with some we might not choose. But if we are willing to stay in His will and draw strength from Him to fulfill His purpose, we'll be blessed and be used to bless others—just as Joy was.

As iron sharpens iron, so one man sharpens another (Proverbs 27:17).

CONSIDER THIS

Are there people in your life you're finding difficult? What about them puts you off? Can you see how God might use them to grow and bless you? If not, will you ask God to show you, and use you to bless them too?

Pumpkin Can't Wait

God's Timing Is Perfect

Avoid being impatient. Remember time brings roses.

Author Unknown

Pumpkin was a big cat. That explained his ability to stand with his hind feet on the floor and reach the dining room table with his front paws. Whenever I served his favorite foods, such as fish or chicken, he would beg in this inventive way. Not that he needed to because we've always given our cats scraps under the table. But Pumpkin wasn't content to curl up and wait patiently for his treat. Hoping to hurry up the process, he'd plant his front paws on the table and stare hungrily at his humans—for as long as it took.

The guests at our table usually had a good laugh at Pumpkin's impatience. We house foreign students, and their response was always the same; to run for their camera so they could capture how this cat looked forever! Pumpkin was not deterred in his quest to hurry up the feeding process, so most people who wanted a photo got one, and we're certain Pumpkin is famous the world over for this.

Pumpkin didn't just stand passively with his front paws at the edge of the table. Every so often he'd nudge someone's hand with his paw to try to get food faster. We didn't mind his tap on our hands. We understood that he just wanted to speed up the pace a bit.

Sometimes we act just like Pumpkin with our gracious heavenly Father. We try to nudge His hand to give us what He has for us just a little bit quicker. In our eagerness, we push for our timing rather than His, and He must teach us to wait on Him—as He did with Laurel.

Laurel came to Jesus about three years ago as a young adult, and she took off like a rocket in her faith. She became very active in her church and joined several Bible studies because she wanted to catch up for all the lost years without Jesus. She has since grown in her faith and now serves with the youth. She loves that God has her life in His hands. Recently she became attracted to a godly man at her church, and she began to pray about him because he fit every one of the criteria on her list for a husband. He showed some interest in her as well, so when they began to do things together, she was elated, thinking God was answering her prayers. As they talked more and became closer, Laurel began to push for the relationship to become more than just a friendship. This had been her MO with men in her pre-Christian days. As she pushed harder, this young man pulled back…more and more. Finally he began to avoid her, even moving to the far side of a room when she entered it. She got the message, backed way off, and decided he wasn't the one after all. As her heart healed she began to realize that God was trying to teach her not to be the mover and shaker she had been before she met Him, but to wait on His timing, which would be perfect. She recognized that she couldn't nudge God's hand into getting what she wanted any sooner. Laurel is now trusting God to bring her whomever He has for her, whether it is this man or another.

God understands our struggles. He understands that we desire to know what He has for us on the table of our lives. I don't think

God minds at all that we stretch up to see because we are acknowledging Him as the owner of our lives, the giver of good things. And He uses our nudging to help us learn to trust His timing and release our agenda and wait on His.

I've done a lot of waiting in my life since I became a Christian many years ago. I see this now as God building my faith in Him. He has taught me to wait on His timing instead of nudging His hand—as He did when I wanted to teach a Bible study class.

I knew God had given me the gift of teaching. I was in a Bible study that was part of a national program. I thought I had heard God tell me He wanted me to begin a new class in Los Angeles and help teach it. I prayed for Him to show me when it was to happen. In the meantime, I waited instead of tapping His hand. I didn't tell anyone but my husband, and for me that's a big deal! There was even a period when I thought perhaps I had heard God wrong. I wrote in my journal, "It's okay if You don't have a class for me to teach. I am content in what You do have for me now."

And then one day as I was driving home from a speaking engagement, the Lord spoke one word to my heart: "Now." I was so excited I could hardly wait to tell my best friends. They came along to help start this new class, which is now in its eighteenth year. I had heard God correctly after all!

God has things for each of us on the table of our lives. Sometimes He gives us a peek at them. Sometimes He doesn't. God gave David a peek when he was anointed as a youth to be Israel's future king. Many years would pass before David was crowned. He could have tried to hurry things up, but he didn't. He waited on God. And God not only fulfilled that promise, He gave David a new one: "Your house and your kingdom will endure forever before me; your throne will be established forever" (2 Samuel 7:16).

For all his paw-tapping, Pumpkin only got table scraps. God desires to give us so much more. He knows not only *what* is best, but *when*. And He always has our best interests at heart. So release your agenda, trust His timing, and wait patiently on Him.

Many, O LORD my God, are the wonders you have done. The things you planned for us no one can recount to you; were I to speak and tell of them, they would be too many to declare (Psalm 40:5).

CONSIDER THIS

Have you ever had to wait on the Lord for something He put on your heart? What struggles did you have? Were you tempted to take things into your own hands? If you did, what happened? If you didn't, what helped you resist? How did this experience build your faith?

Separation Anxiety

God Finds Those We Can't

When prodigals return
great things are done.

A.A. Dowty

The cheery chirp of my instant mail belied the grim message on my computer. Leia the cat had gone missing! She and her brother, Luke (named for the famous *Star Wars* characters), belonged to close friends of mine. They'd been adopted from a rescue group and welcomed into a cat-loving family complete with two children to spoil and adore them. They'd been safe. But now Leia had strayed and her people were panicked.

My friends live north of Sunset Boulevard in a hilly section of L.A. All kinds of critters roam there, including coyotes. Luke and Leia were not allowed outside for this reason. But this day my friends had rushed off to a meeting, leaving a door to their backyard unlatched. It was windy. The door had blown open, and Leia got out. They knew this because when they returned, the man who serviced their pool was there and had seen her dashing back and forth along their fence.

Any cat-lover knows an agile feline can escape from enclosures dogs and humans can't. My frantic friends had searched their large yard for an hour. They had roamed their immediate neighborhood, calling Leia's name in hopes she'd answer. They could find no trace of their small gray cat. And while she'd been microchipped, Leia had no tags or collar. There was no outward sign of where she lived…no address or phone number to call. But that was the least of her humans' worries. When darkness fell, the coyotes came out. This small, inexperienced cat stood no chance against a formidable foe she didn't even know existed. "If she's still out there after dusk, she's dead," my friends wailed.

I went to help. I tromped through their ivy, calling Leia too. Their kids got home from school and joined the hunt. We all felt awful, even Luke, who'd mewed plaintively until being shut up in a room so his family could leave house doors open in hopes his sister might wander back inside.

That didn't happen. As daylight dimmed, my friends made "missing cat" flyers. I left as they were preparing to go door to door. I'd prayed. I'd asked other friends to pray. "I don't know what else I can do," I said. "Only God can find Leia." At these words, the kids' mother swallowed hard and cast her eyes pleadingly toward heaven.

Back home I begged God to answer our prayers. "If Leia's not dead, please bring her home for the kids' sake. I know You can work this miracle if You choose." I went out to dinner and ran some errands, returning late. My phone's message light was blinking. Leia was found!

My friends had heard meowing and gone out to check. Their garage door won't go down completely. Leia must have seen the light within and squeezed through the gap. They found her hiding inside. Their poor little cat was covered with foliage and seemed petrified.

Leia's experience made me ponder what happens when God's children stray from Him. I have many Christian friends who are moms or dads. Some have seen a grown son or daughter wander from the faith of their youth through an unlatched door. What blew the door open varied: the lure of this world, humanistic philosophies, doubts, disappointment because of a seemingly unanswered prayer. Whatever the cause, these young men and women left their spiritual home. And their loved ones agonized, knowing that a spiritual coyote was lurking outside. First Peter 5:8 warns, "Your enemy the devil prowls around like a roaring lion looking for someone to devour." Even though my friends believed that no one who truly belongs to God can be lost in an eternal sense, they knew their children risked untold hazards and grief.

And so these parents "called" their children, as my friends did Leia the cat. They invited the strays to Bible studies or to church. They tried to talk to them about God. But like Leia, some of these wanderers didn't respond. And the parents were tempted to panic.

But just as God knew where to find Leia, He knows where to find these spiritual strays. Only He knows what will bring them back. Only He can save them from harm and lead them squeezing under the garage door. Our part is not to nag or badger, but to plead for them in prayer.

A friend of mine did this. She pleaded in prayer for her oldest son for many years. He'd asked Jesus into his heart as a child. He had been baptized at his own request. He was in the youth group at his church and went to services regularly. But in his college years, he began to stray. God became less central in his life. The lure of this world blew open his unlatched door. Once he was married, he rarely went to church, except on special holidays.

My friend was concerned. She called her son, but she didn't badger him. Instead, she prayed fervently to the One who could find him. Years passed. The son saw his sister and brother-in-law develop a vibrant faith in Christ. One weekend, their own young boy was baptized and the whole family attended. The child's faith touched my friend's son deeply. The pastor's message grabbed him too. He felt the Lord tug on his heart. Not long afterward, he seized the chance to go with his brother-in-law and a church team to minister in New Orleans for a week. He saw God work in amazing ways. He joyfully squeezed back under the garage door, his flickering faith ignited again.

On that awful night when Leia was lost, after all the cat fliers were given out, my friends' ten-year-old daughter closed herself in her room. She knelt at the foot of her bed and begged God for her cat. When Leia was found, my friends awakened both children, and that little girl rejoiced in the miracle of God's restoration.

How much more does God long to restore His strays to the safety of His fold. Though their will can resist Him, our prayers can battle for them. So pray for strays, watch what God will do, and rejoice in His power and love.

The father said to his servants, "Quick! Bring the best robe and put it on him. Put a ring on his finger and sandals on his feet. Bring the fattened calf and kill it. Let's have a feast and celebrate. For this son of mine was dead and is alive again; he was lost and is found." So they began to celebrate (Luke 15:22-24).

CONSIDER THIS

Do you have loved ones who have strayed from God? What are your concerns for them? How might you call them while entrusting God to find them?

Jericho Moments

Watch for Glimpses of God

The world is full of wonders and miracles but man takes his little hand and covers his eyes and sees nothing.

RABBI ISRAEL BAAL SHEM TOV

What's the difference between a coincidence and a glimpse of God? Sometimes the label depends on one's perspective. There are those who would say the way I got my new kitty, Bo, was happenstance. I prefer to see it as a "Jericho moment."

I'd been wanting another boy cat ever since losing Merlin, my orange tabby, to cancer in late summer of 2005. I had two very senior kitties and a female Ragdoll a decade younger. Over my lifetime, my animal family has included both mixed breeds and purebreds. This time I wanted another Ragdoll, preferably a flame point in honor of Merlin's coloring. But, for a variety of reasons, I wasn't sure this was God's timing.

Still, I trolled the Internet, checking various sites. I found some flame point kittens located not far from my home. I liked what I saw but had no peace about moving forward, so I held off.

Time passed. I was now working on the manuscript for this book. I still wanted a cat and kept checking the web for Ragdolls of various colors. Around Christmas of 2006, I decided to inquire about an older kitten I sparked to. But the due date for our book was approaching. I felt that introducing a new cat to my multipet household wasn't something I could handle on deadline. I prayed they'd hold him if this was right. They wouldn't. The kitten was taken.

In odd moments over the next weeks, I e-mailed other inquiries. None panned out. I kept praying, wrestling with my will versus God's. Maybe I was just trying to force things, and this wasn't supposed to happen. And then one inquiry triggered a positive response. An older male flame point Ragdoll kitten was available. I asked for a picture. When I saw it, I fell in love. I'd already chosen a name—Bo. Could this be the kitty that went with it?

As I asked more questions, other things started falling into place. His temperament sounded just right for my situation. He was already neutered too, which I felt was a plus. And the timing of getting him was "purr-fect." Bo was living in another state, but a friend of his current owner could bring him to me in early April. This was past my book deadline and right around my birthday.

I still had some lingering doubts. Was this more my idea than God's? I spoke with a friend who knew me and my situation well. She said it seemed this little guy was the right cat at the right time. She urged me to go for it, praying and trusting God would halt the process if I'd misread the matter. Instead, He gave me one last marvelous confirmation, out of nowhere.

I'd been told that Bo was about eight months of age. He turned out to be a bit more. His owner e-mailed that he'd be a year old on March 19. I happened to mention this when I e-mailed a photo of him to our editor contact at our publishing house. I nearly fell off my chair when I received her reply. This was her birthday too!

My heart leaped. It felt like a "Jericho moment"—a supernatural glimpse of God. No way could I have orchestrated this! What were the odds of Bo having the same birthday as anyone I knew—let alone *this* person? I felt God had given me a small miracle to confirm His blessing on getting this cat and affirm He loved me and was working in my life.

God did the same thing for my friend Rachel—not over a cat, but a home. Rachel raised two kids as a single mom, struggling to make ends meet on a modest paycheck. Fortunately, the house she rented didn't cost much. But suddenly, after 18 years, she was told the owner was selling and she had to find a new place to live.

Added to the jolt of leaving her home, Rachel experienced major sticker shock when she started checking prices in the housing rental market. What's more, she'd inherited her now grown children's dog. This narrowed her housing options further. Because she was allergic to the dog, she'd gladly have found it another home, but there seemed no prospects for that, either.

Rachel loved the Lord. In herself, she felt helpless, but she grabbed onto Him. She prayed. She looked for a new place. She found nothing affordable that she liked. As time ticked down to her moving deadline, I told her she and her dog could come stay with me temporarily till she found something. Other friends advised her to settle for what she could get right then and be done, but she felt God leading otherwise. She shoved her possessions into storage and came to my house.

More time passed. Other pressures imploded, and she wasn't doing much looking. But she was praying about her new home, and what it would have. When she did look at places, she felt God saying, "Wait."

And then one day when she was walking with her closest friend, they spied a rental sign—right across from her friend's small duplex. It was for a house behind a house. No one was there, and Rachel felt certain the place would cost more than she could pay. But at her friend's urging, they checked back the next day. They met the landlord—who was waiting for someone else to come see the unit. It had everything Rachel wanted, and amazingly, it was in her price range.

Rachel thought she had gotten her dream. But my own heart sank. Her prospective new home was a no-pet deal. I'd once offered to keep her dog for a while if the place she found wouldn't take it, but I had two dogs and four cats of my own, and after some weeks with her dog in my house, I'd realized a seventh animal would be overload. I dreaded telling her. She understood, but she was crushed. At my suggestion, she offered her landlord more money to let the dog come with her. He said no and told her someone else was also interested in the place.

The next few days were dark for us both. I tried not to be consumed with guilt. She tried to get up the gumption to start looking again. We prayed. Others prayed. And then another friend of Rachel's called. She offered to take Rachel's dog as a pal for her own pooch.

Rachel was glad, but she figured it was too late to grab the place she had wanted. Surely it had been rented by now. I said, "Call anyway." When she did, she learned the other renters had fallen through. The house was there. It was hers. To this day, she calls this a "Jericho moment" in her life.

As you may know, the original Jericho was a famous walled city of the Canaanites. It seemed impregnable, but God gave Joshua and the Israelites a plan to conquer it (Joshua 6). The plan was odd, to say the least. God told them to march silently around the city for seven days. On the last day, when they had done this, their priests were to blow on trumpets while the people shouted loudly. God said if they did this, the city's walls would fall down—and they did!

It was a miracle. It was a sign that God had won the victory. It was a glimpse of His supernatural power. It was a way to build their faith and affirm His love, His blessing, and His working in their lives.

A cat and an editor with the same birthday, a new home provided against all odds, city walls that crumbled to trumpet blasts and shouts. All are sightings of God at work in our lives in supernatural ways. But I wonder how many such "Jericho moments" we miss because we simply aren't watching for them. We live in a culture that tempts us to over-rationalize everything, even God, and if we do, these glimpses of Him may slip past us unrecognized.

God is waiting to give us "Jericho moments" if we have eyes to see. So watch for them, that your doubts may topple and your faith in Him prevail.

Your ways, O God, are holy. What god is so great as our God? You are the God who performs miracles; you display your power among the peoples (Psalm 77:13-14).

CONSIDER THIS

What Jericho moments have you seen in your life? How did they impact your faith? Do you think, in retrospect, that you may have missed some? How do you see God at work in your life right now in supernatural ways?

CAT TAILS...ER, TALES...BY AUTHOR

M.R. WELLS

CONNIE FLEISHAUER

DOTTIE P. ADAMS

Meet the Authors

M.R. Wells has written extensively for children's animated television, including several Disney shows and the animated PBS series *Adventures from the Book of Virtues.* She has also worked on the live-action video series *Bibleman.* With Kris Young and Connie Fleishauer, she coauthored a devotional for dog lovers, *Four Paws from Heaven.* She lives in Los Angeles and counts herself blessed by the love of her pets, her family, her friends, and her Lord.

Connie Fleishauer is a teacher and writer and enjoys filmmaking. She coauthored *Four Paws from Heaven* with Kris Young and M.R. Wells. With her friends Susie and Cory, she produces films that encourage children to read. Connie is the wife of a Bakersfield, California, farmer, a mother of three grown children, a mother-in-law, and a grandma. She loves life and the One who gave it to her.

Dottie P. Adams is a Teaching Director for Community Bible Study and has taught a Los Angeles-area Bible class for 18 years. She's the wife of a retired physicist whom she adores. She's also the mother of three grown children and a grandma to four. An ardent photographer, she creates annual photo journal albums of her family and has an online photo business with her son-in-law. Dottie has loved cats since childhood and is grateful to God for creating purring creatures who are so beautiful, funny, and endearing.

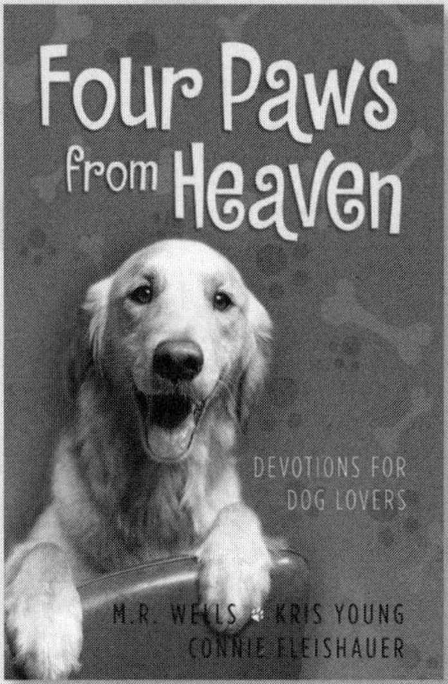

Life is Better with a Dog

Friend, family member, guardian, comforter—a dog can add so much to our lives. These furry, four-footed creatures truly are wonderful gifts from a loving Creator to bring joy, laughter, and warmth to our hearts and homes. Sometimes they do seem "heaven sent."

These delightful devotions will make you smile and perhaps grow a little misty as you enjoy true stories of how God watches over and provides for us even as we care for our canine companions. Experience warm moments of connection with Him as you consider

- how a little obedience can keep you from danger
- why trusting your Master is always a good thing to do
- how just being with God is the best possible place to be